Content

'Secretions of the Beast' was written from an immoral, and insane vantage point. Though its contents are meant to be perceived as works of art, the mission of which intending to be therapeutic, entertaining, relatable, and enjoyed, it may still negatively affect victims of trauma, phobias, and mental illness. The topics included are:
-Sexual Abuse
-Abortion
-Dead Animals
-Sexual Content
-Nudity
-Psychotic Delusion
-Gore
-Drug Use
-Depression/Suicide
-Strong Language
-Demonic Horror

It is intended only for a mature audience. Please do enjoy at your own discretion.
– Thank you,

Emenual Wolff

Madelyn,

thank you endlessly for the support!

Emanuel L. Wolff

Copyright © 2017 by Emenual Wolf, MN Arts.

All rights reserved. This book or any portion thereof may not be reproduced or used in any manner without the written consent of the publisher, except for the use of brief quotations in book review.

SECRET IONS OF THE BEAST

*No, that's not...
that isn't quite right.*

*The **Devil** Made me do it! Fixate on electric lore in plasma pennies, plasma gore, and neural lace in veins. "Secret-ions," what a clever little play on phonemes. The **Devil** made me do it!*

*He wants to pick and pry at temples. He wants to **infect** us with machines.*

What the fuck are you talking about? No, he doesn't –

HE WANTS US
    TO **BEG** FOR OUR
        HUMANITY,
            LESS WE LOAD
IMMORTAL DREAMS
    INTO
            ELECTRIC SHEEP!!

Oh, the book?
I did that. That was me. This. I should say, "this." Not the Devil.
This isn't Satanas Lucifer, ruler of Hell.

This is worse.

Secretions of the BEAST

~~Emenual~~ Wolff

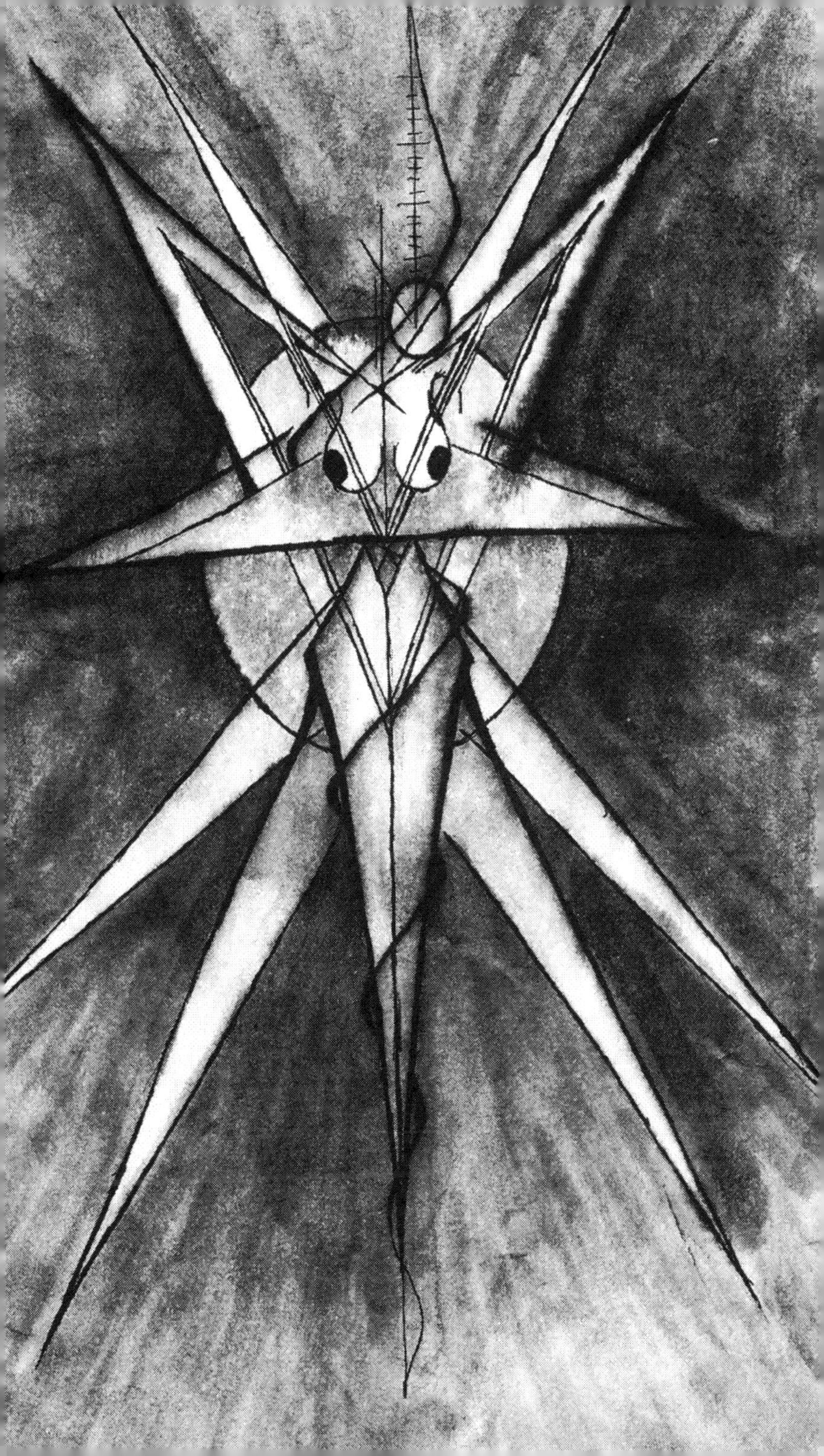

I dedicate these poetic verses to John Searle,
Ed Gein, Albert Camus,
Bonnie Parker, Phillip Mainländer, Charlie
Manson, and Thích Quảng Đức.

How extraordinarily dry, must your soul be, to
see things as they truly are.

Rape me, like angels;

      Infect my head. You will lose. You will lose
this inside voice, antichrist,
inside boy, inside blood,
inside blood.

      Squeeze and swoon the fruits that suicide
slide around the boy, the girl, the blood,
the blood, and
reap me.
I said it; **rape** me! *Sheer* the branches
dripping forbidden brutes and hear me.

That I am not alone.
I am not alone!
I AM *NOT **ALONE***!

Juice the life of lie and exploit my contagion fierce
diamond pierced cancer mind;
I really love to let the lie
use me.
M.Use. Me.

See how far I've cum to die, you orgy; puppet
strings BDSM, vulture mind; you sadist
determinist, so virtuous contagious…

Society *pigs and* psychology *swine*! I'm fine.
                I'M *FINE!*
Emulate my happy crime of orgasm life inside the
lie and **NEVER. STOP.** ~~**RAPING**~~. **ME**.
    "When all of your wishes are granted, many of
        your dreams will be destroyed."

An Empty Cup;

What am I to do? I'm to stand?
I'm to stand on the cusp of optimistic hopeful cliffs,
which overhang an ocean of oblivion;
all the spinning tides of time…
      So many more before me have died. So many more than alive. For the majority of my existence I'll be dead.
      So. Fucking. Dead.
And you'll never know just how animated it is to be dead. As cells and atoms and quirks irk to shrink and grow I too can spread. Still us, alive, 'cognizant' of fleeting time, us CREATURES *PAY NO MIND* to the ever-ended; past the mourns, barring memorials…

      I'd let death be my teacher if I had the motivation. For its eternal world of nature will harbor me much longer than our own. Compared to death, our life is as long as a muffled scream. Compared to death, our life is as long as the
                                  blip
of a   question mark
          ?

                    Damned.

      DAMN this spirit mutiny, and DAMN the body to which it's abandoned me, and DAMN my thoughts of the world, of the girl, and all the faces I drool to see. DAMN ALL THE PLACES I RUN TO, just to flee. I don't ever *want* to stay, and I don't know how to be. Just be.

> I DON'T KNOW HOW TO BE.

This terror of time, it grinds my mind and I'm too blind to find any kind of validity.

> So, what am I to do? Am I to stand? Just stand
> and let this happen on the sacred grounds of reality?
>> Those heretic, heathen, optimist casualties; the holy monuments of life's greatest gifts and beauty; the utmost prized possession of natural positivity; all these sacred, sacred lands of God given reality...

> I hate you, me.
> I
> Hate
> You.

Because you'll never let me see what it's like to be obliterated.

> No one ever does, and how I wish Death would teach me better, in this oxymoronic short, long life.

See? Every Nothing;

Don't think about it.
I want to die.
I. Want. To. Die.

Because I can. I can do anything;
I'm annihilation; a conversation of creation;
every nothing.

See? Every Nothing.

I am God, and I want to die.
Through drink, and lust, in thought;
from dust to dust, and art betwixt
the spaces of space-time.
I am just. Not, "a just God," but
Just. A. God.
A life like no other nightmare afore.
Cold, alone, bored,
alone
in a void so empty it hasn't even happened yet.
An astronaut with center data, not mass.
I am not; I am.
I did not, yet do. Don't. Do.
Don't – think about it.
I want to fucking die.
Because I can. I am Just.
A. God.
I must "be," if I'm to pass.

Arcade;

In the aura of Hell, I contract a subtle emulation.
How envious my heart pleads me not be,
    that maybe much like you,
        I could know our gold coin;
        I should taste our comfort;
        accept your clever guise and
invitation,
into the devious lands of "milk, and honey."
    That maybe, much like you, I could pretend.
Of all the faces and all the fame, that only I could
feel the shame of who I was and who I am.
Selling even the nostalgic remembering, of when I
used to say,

        "Of souls in coins, we live to pay.

        *We have to **WANT***
            *to **HAVE** to play."*

Now I say nothing,

    and play nowhere,

        but watch the termites

    eat their world away.

Oh how I love to watch them feed on this arcade.

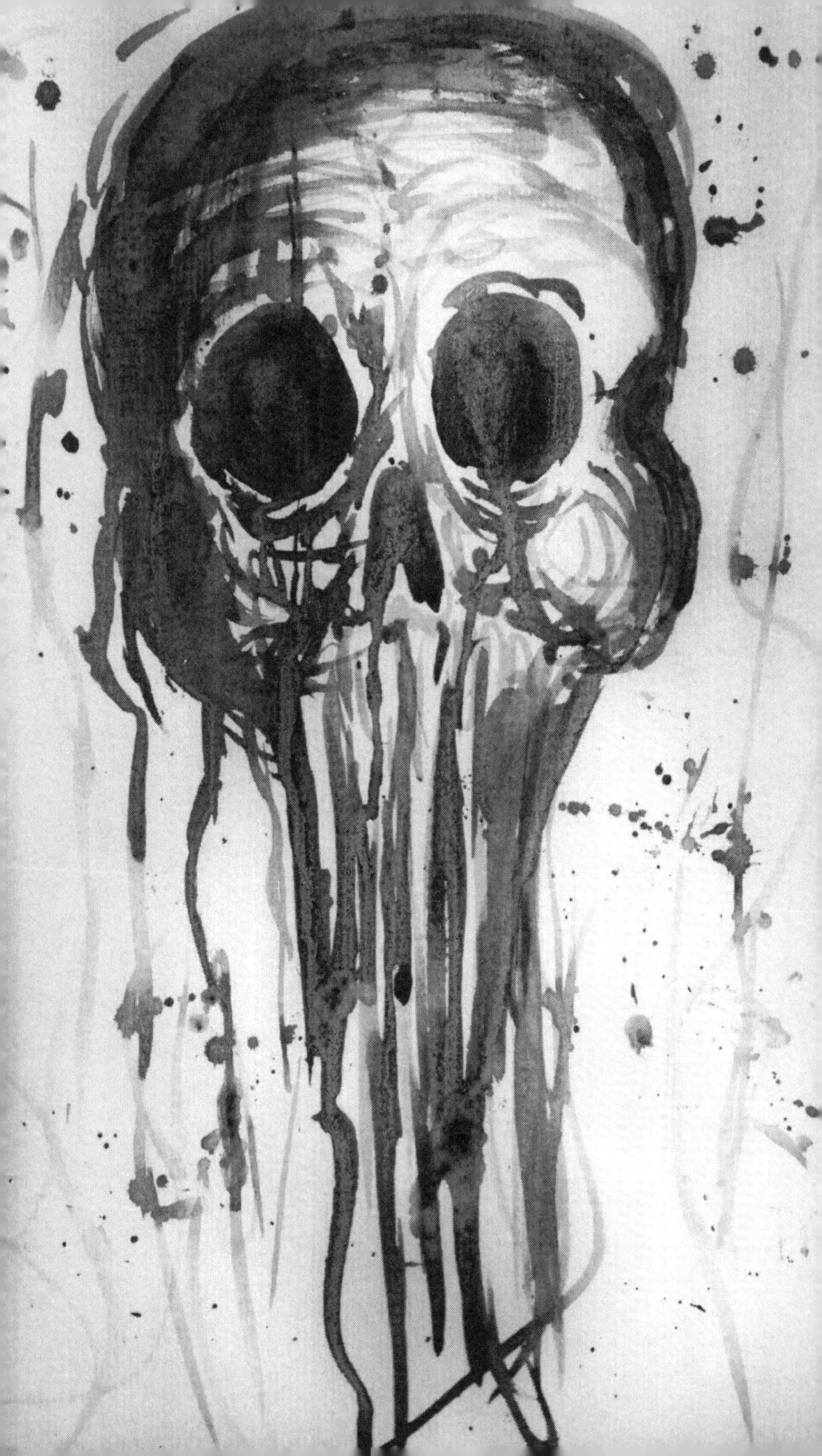

Never Nowhere;

This must be the greatest joke ever sold.
    'Why do you care?'
    That's what Albert Camus asks. That's
what any Nihilist asks.
Why the fuck does one feel obliged to ask?
    Just ask Nietzsche. Or Hitler. Or don't.

I care but I know that I shouldn't.
I shouldn't be or feel or do anywhere. I should not.
Yet it already happened, and I'm already here.
There is no sanctity of this.
No reason.
I'm rambling, and it seems senseless but in this
senseless fucking world,
    does that even matter?

I already found a 'where' and 'when.' I already
thought it up, in real-time; but a 'why?'
This choice I've made; it can't be turned around.

That's what they say: "It can't be turned around."
    ...
'Hate' is such a strong word.
It makes no difference in death.
    I hate you.

It makes no difference in life either.
    I need you.
    Don't you dare do this; don't
    you dare
    leave me here alone.

Bettering;

This is the life on worlds end. The yearn for
something more when
so much is given.
This is the edge of the pill,
the crave of the blade,
the fucking
dripless itch
of the endless facade.

I just want to sleep when I know I should.
I just want to eat when
I'm hungry.
I just want to know how to do this.
I'm sorry.

Meet My Tomb;

Maybe
you're not the one who's
dreaming;
Maybe you're not the one
who's dead.
Of these sorrow times my eyes are reaping,
in all the sight
and sound
and sense I've bled.
A grand intrusive hound
with ways of words; the spirits
bound to living.

Let's get high as a tomb, flip your world
upside down,
watch the clouds fall from the sky,
to tumble 'round to death.

All the Monsters We Birth;

Genetic lucidity; wildly genetic… genes of the wild lunatic realm; these epigenetic Gene Wilder sounds.

"LIFE! Life do you hear me?! Give my creation life!"

Biological tones with frequency DNA. Deoxyribonucleic acid spells the design.
After all, God "said" let there be light. There first was the word; the soundscape of endless nothings to echo within, apart of and then
never to hear fully, or see, but be. Just be.

Where are we again? Floating in solidarity on a time line that bends onto itself – floating on a rock in the thing that both is, and allows the chance of other things to be.

Where and when is *NOW* when 'now' is 80 milliseconds slipped through the powers of processing.

"LIFE! LIFE DO YOU HEAR ME?!"

I'm not so sure that you do. Why would this birth of sight cease my choice to cut my throat or continue? I need to see you see me;
> eyes within heads, within eyes; observers
> observed – please! Give me life!

Skin on skin

to touch and be read. Souls dance with souls under skin, over red blood and cream-colored bones, and wires of minds primordial, and bold; they scream to be fucked and listened to.
They scream to be told they're worth listening to. Am I worth being bought, and held, and loved? Because,
        we are our own creations, but we never had this choice. A polaroid life line and one ceaseless yearning voice –

GOD DAMNIT, I LOVE YOU!!

        I think that's what it means…
To love, and be loved. After all, I'm your creation as much as you are your own.

"Life! Life do you hear me?! Give my creation life!"

Because,
        truth is impossible, morality is arbitrary, the flow of time is an illusion, reality is a reconstructed hallucination that we'll never see outside of, and
        I
                Love
                          You.

See? I love you.

Entering;

Sewn in button bones,
unspoken gravity polaroid's, and lifelong dreams.

You fuse a moment, endlessly; a gasp in motion,
you fuse to me,
with child wide eyes and curiosity.
Be still like broken glass, and hold me close, my
'endlessly.'

Because you're about to start again, and
it'll hurt
like no other time before.
A black hole multiverse morality reborn.

Clean as a mist is the transition,
once it's passed.
A lone,
long note
in a violins cry; an ocean
as deep as alien skies;
the stinging path of life emulates.

I've no advice for you, old soul,
but to brace.
Brace.
Brace.
Begin again, and brace.

Abort-ions;

It must be this investment, or feeling of,
which keeps me here at all.
        Am I afraid?
Afraid
of what I'll see if I were to look outside...
    Dear child heed, don't. Don't look at the sky.
There's evil in the mud,
               and of the summer greens
        they cry,
"It's best you stay safe
        and inside."

Maybe it's here this will end.
      I could die, you know.
          I could finish

now.

You should've let me finish then. **WHY THE *FUCK* DID YOU BRING ME HERE?!** **WHY** didn't you vacuum me out of these pupil wombs? Your dilated cervices should vomit this font from their essence and never return. **NEVER RETURN TO THIS PAGE!**

Why? Because I've *told you so*, and so has everyone else in your life. Childhood through adolescence, until it's so programmed in the brain that even now you find yourself filling the mouths of babes with warnings of dark corners and pathology.

NEVER

      RETURN

           TO THIS **PAGE**

Less your mind will learn the magic of powering down. That it's unarguably better to have never been. ***Why didn't you let me end?!***

      Here, let me start over...

SECRETIONS OF THE BEAST

— MN UAL WOLFF

Memorize;

    Every day I came, I thought you'd be dead. I suppose I'll see you when I'm not fucking around. They say you see your life in the eyes of those who love you. I see my death in yours;
    I love you too.

Yes, the book. The book, and the knife. The knife and the posted grail; all hail, the ultimate choice is up to the unwitting doe,

Just,   not   when   it   comes   to   you.

I'm powerless to you.

    So blow your load of termite bones and watch them eat away my chest. I won't pretend to have any shame. I'll suck your maggots free to eat the rest of all I have to give or blame.
    This divine solitude.
    That maybe one has endured this wickedness, but they are not like me. They did not do this to themselves; they did not forgive you.

    Forgive you, for giving me the nightmare; die.
    Forgive me for forgiving you;
DIE.

    I'll let me be used, so I can use you too; die.

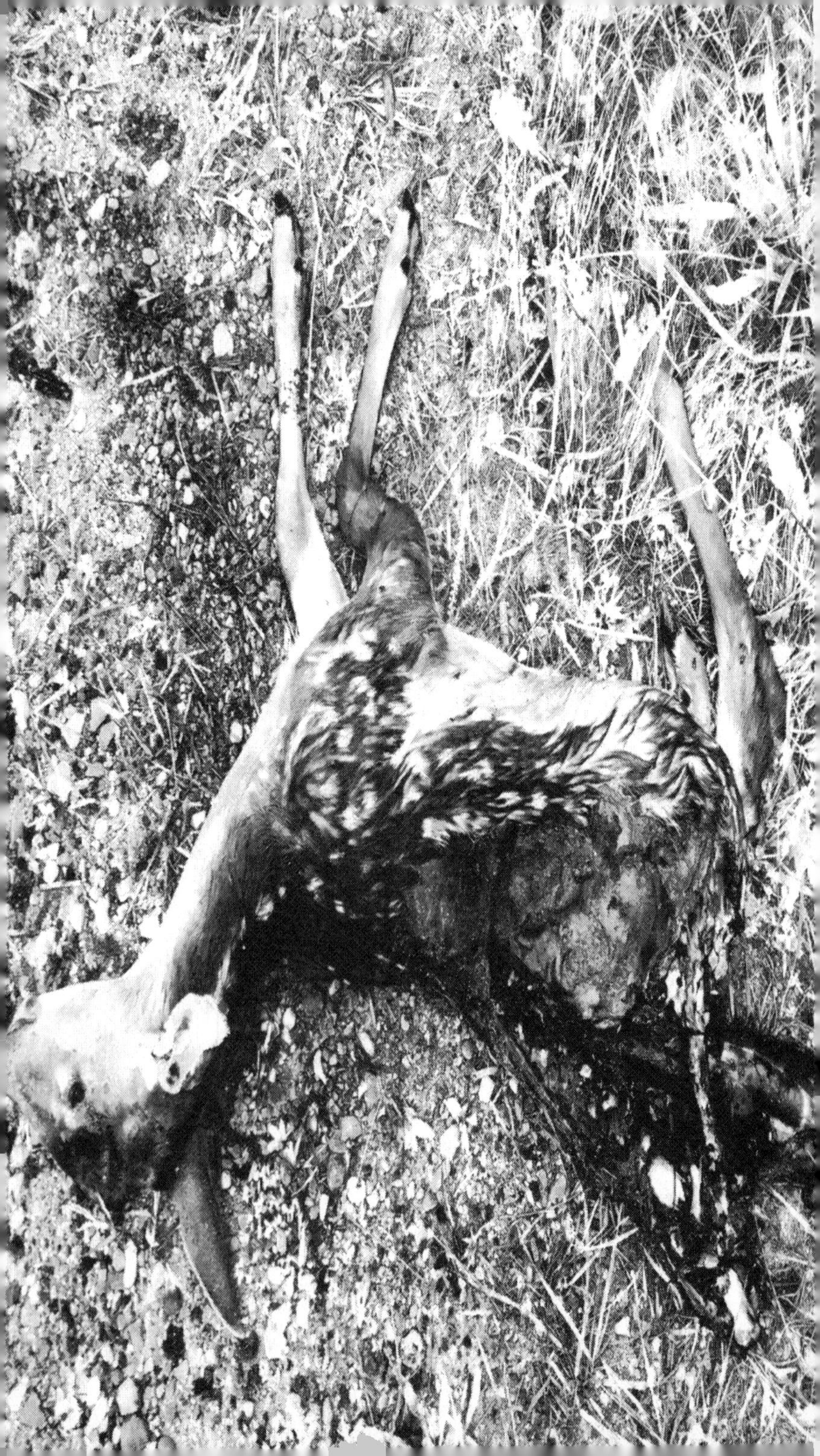

Every Little Nothing;

It's okay to be every nothing.
To fill up the spaces between
dads arm chair

         and moms drying rack.
To take up the time
between love,
      and a new car,
           and the family dog,
                and your brother's death.

It's okay to be
Every Nothing.
Because,
      that's where the sweet spot is;
where there's chance.
That maybe ***this*** will matter.

I am in every nothing –
the idea you forgot you had.
    The dream you'll never love to live again.
      The piece of you, you left with me,
that after so much time had passed I began
to believe it was myself.

    This is the cry of Every Nothing:
that
"<u>**MAYBE . THIS . WILL . MATTER.**</u>
    *Let me combust into a gasp, let me catch
your holy eye; I will be what matters.*

Let me swirl into a flame, let me lick your palms with sweat; I will be what matters.
Let me dance inside your blood, and spill it on what's left; see?
I will be what matters.
Let me cut you like a blade shaves skin from sacred fruit and remind me that
This. Fucking. Matters."

So that when it's free, is after we've agreed its
death. A moment, they call it;
a breath that's come to pass.
That in every little nothing
Is something that could last…

"It is okay to be Every Nothing."

A Pet;

Feed me pills and gouge out my eyes.
Don't let me see it, just
put it in me.
Feed me pill after potion,
after
synthetic emotion because I'm so ravished in
hunger.
Tongue wide and submitted, like a churches
collection plate; I can survive anything but this.

How long
until I break my skull open
underneath a credit card
and lighter?

Over and over I pound; over
and over
until my will is nothing more
than sand on alarmist beaches.
Until my teeth
have been transformed into
the blackest of leaches.

How long
until I care
that this will kill me?

Eve all;

Find me

in the poppy fields, emulating
eyes, regurgitating moans,
imitating the smile of a rose bloom;

like the tide of time you boon from me,
I'll be the one
who washed away...

For I am so wet in animal love,
and I've yet
to shove a single fiber back,
but hack into this animal drug
without any fear. Without any fear.

A biological addiction, an infesting bug,
a psychological condition;
you've arrested me.
A pain that's worth the sight to see; see? You've
arrested me, little poppy
tea.

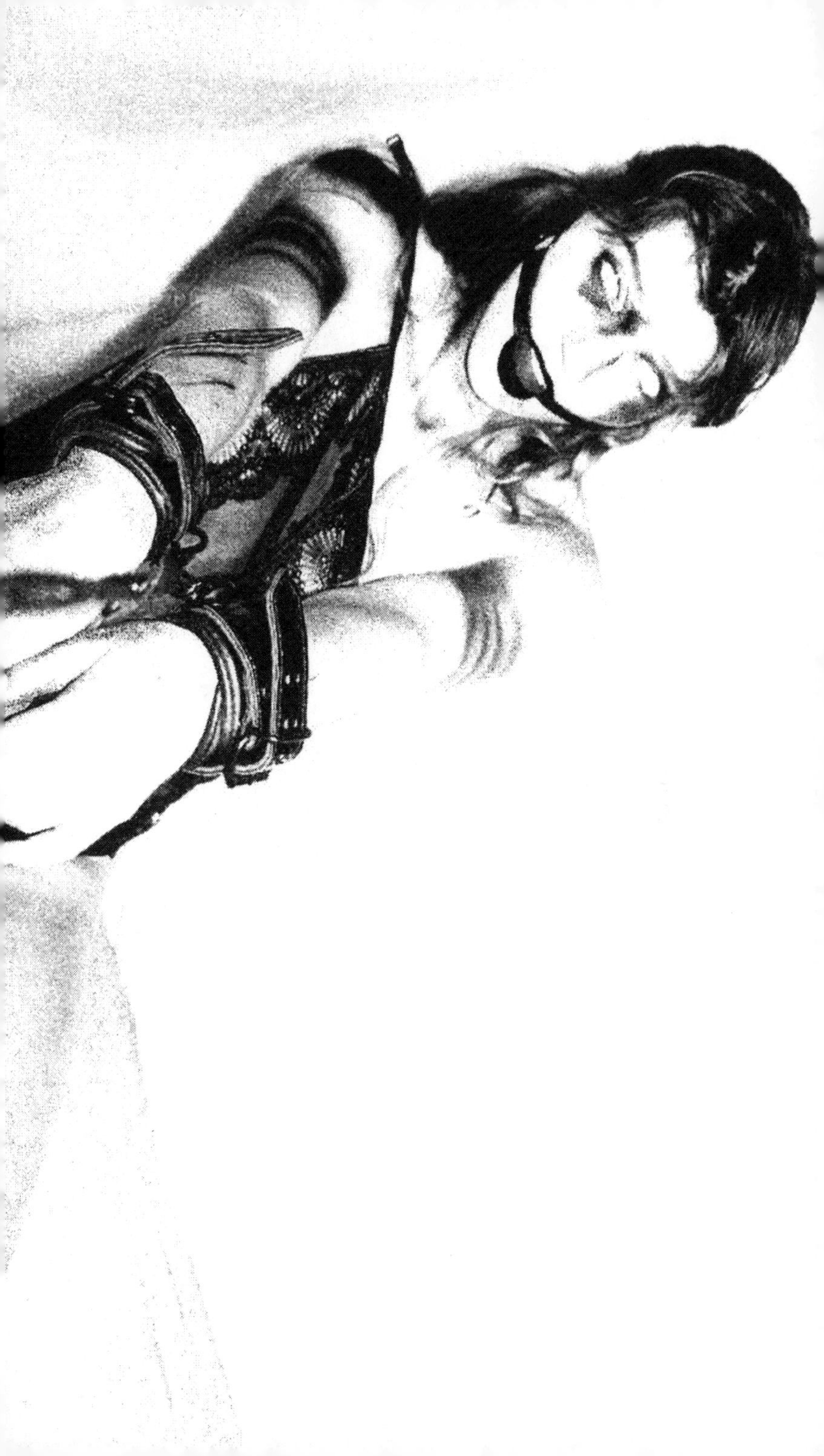

Sex-ed;

Help me find a way to pass the light…

In moans and drinks; in spit and kinks;
we're masters of the night.
You can wear me
with accessories, and flaunt me like design.
You can rob my heart the luxury of giving me your time.
I
used to buy beloved roses; for you,
I'll commit a crime.
Just help me pass this "something" by.

I don't want your sorrow, or
endless narrow figured dime,
but serotonin still infests the etches of my spine.
I know that I don't need you, Letter,
for you're but another line,
and in this book of selfish reason you're the
furthest thing from mine.

So,
I'm greedy, and unwanted;
I'm this pattern paradigm and humble haughty fight.
In all the lessons you could teach me,
help me pass through way
and light.

Place;

Untie my back with razor laughs and gossip ribbon sheers. I'm undressed in betrayal.
Drowning in panic gasps and nightmare baths of solidarity. Shall we grow past such tribal fears of social inability?
Oh, to be alone... to be alone in a smile, and a moment lingered full. Am I okay on my own?
To be alone like some rotten feeble gourd.
To be. Just be. Alone.
Is there a better place to prick your finger, and watch the blood pollute your eyes?
A needle moving slowly, surely into each elbow joint.
Suffer, chained by foreign cries, and ceaseless hallow metal points;
it pokes and pries, the senseless life;
it demands you find your reason.
The nightmare lies of senseless life dilutes it with a motion of will.
A point of commotion; chaos so still.

Still, yes, be still,
that maybe you may find your reason.
That maybe you may know.
Maybe you are God this season,
and God was so alone.
So we
draw baths to taste soap and semen
and sway the tides of steam with joy.

So God drew angels, and gave us reason,
to bend himself into his toys
and die
eternally.
So our orgasms burst in flares across
a moment the size of every space,
and we die within ourselves by
witnessing HIS face;
are we alone?
We give what's left to each other
and each end is frayed
with polar colors
to dilute
and mix
and smear.

untie my back with razor laughs and orgastic
ribbon sheers. I'm undressed,
for you.
Still, I'm alone, and open wide,
and broke inside,
in you.
So very deep, in you.

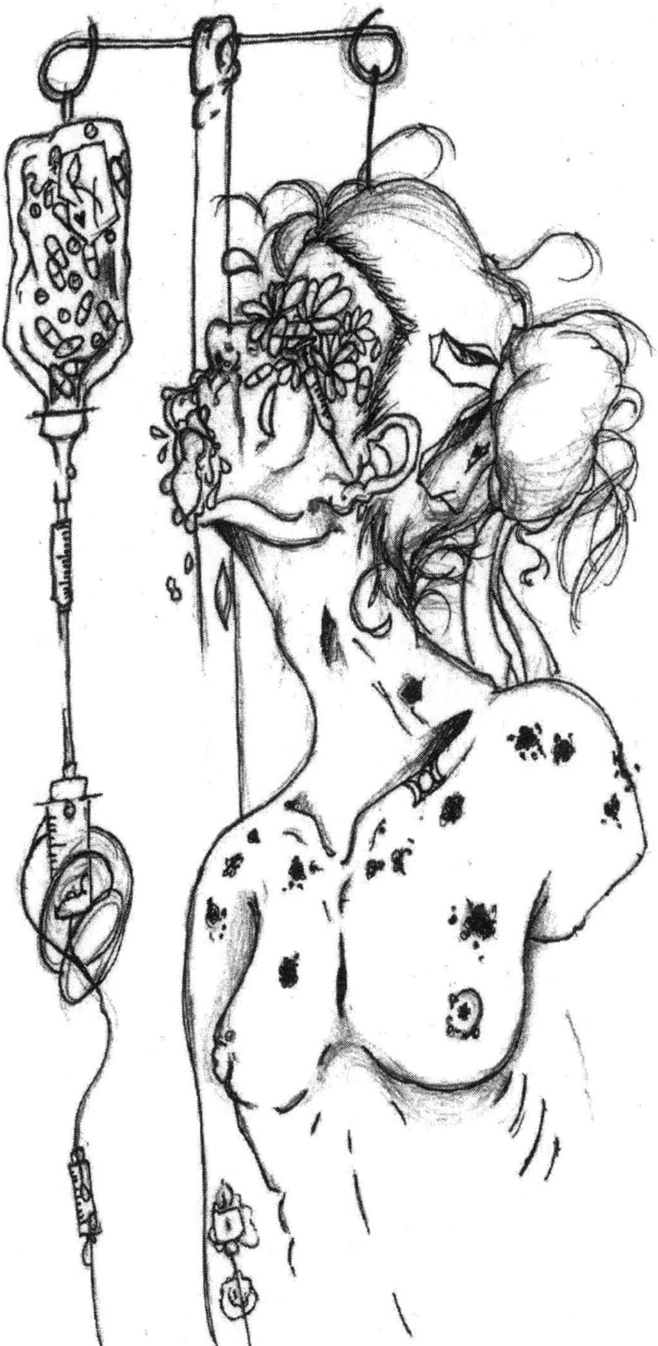

LS Deja-You;

Ticket flames, soaked of gums,
to see the night and all its suns.
Let's get high as a tomb,
       and shake like autumn leaves;
             let the sun rise in soon
to explode its dry light
       and crumble us to slumber.

Lets count ties of our stems,
and smiles like numbers,
to forgive and forget our
sanity woes.

Faith;

I had planned to die young,
        to do it all now
                and see myself through.
See? I had planned
        to die young,
                like you told me to do.

Your dreams will dim,
        your heart won't last long,
this isn't forever son, but, at least you have
your health...
                take me as proof,
        this brutal truth;
die. Young.
Save yourself.

        ...I promise I meant to...

This Dimension has Corners;

She entered me before, her warm and humid breath. She told me to be curious;
>> too real to know.
>> If only I knew…
> A trick against sisters
> and lovers, the umbilical
chains, tightening faster steadfast.
 She unclothed our nakedness with force.
I am enslaved by her incessant breath;
>> life.

In its show was Popobawa; in its script was Asmodeus; in this dance was horror and it has danced in endlessness.
So like a mountain range of
> mirrors with depth
I peer unto the nuclear wasteland;
>> the unfolded dreams.

> I snarl at the injustice of repetition.

Do Not Put Me Back In There.

>> A womb is as dark
>> and grotesque
>> as the egg
>> of a parasite.

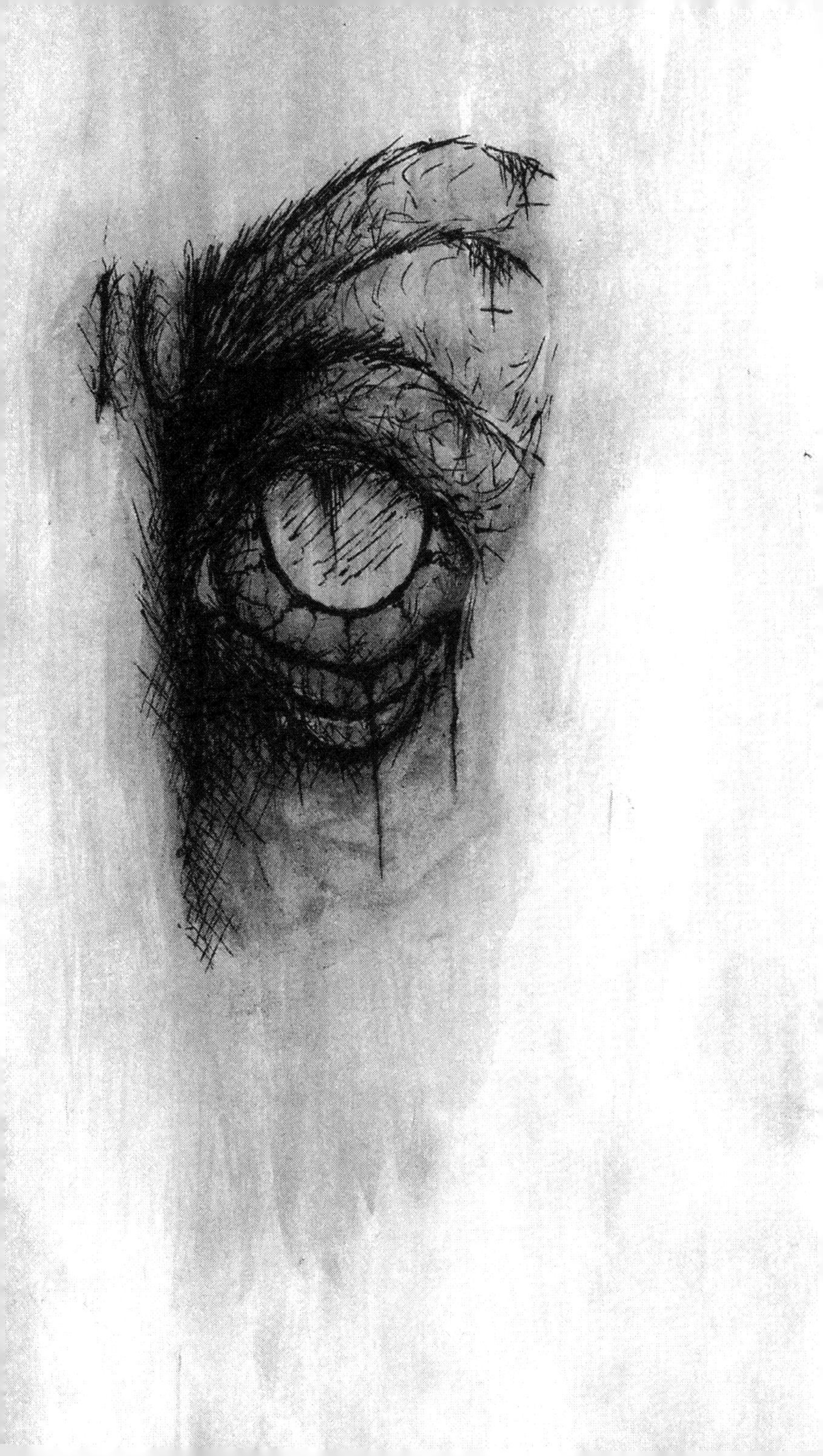

Don't Follow Me;

I enjoy my world of night.
I savor the sweet spaces I find,
that aren't only for the day.
People...
              People... they can be so confused,
and thus,
              confusing.

The sweetest space I've yet to be,
is a place that'll never be
their way.

These daydreams
              can be nightmares...

These daydreams, can be.
They really can be...
These day dreams can be...

Night-Mirrors;

I don't care.
How high you are.
Just so long as you drink me,
and your whiskey,
before my mind see's you full;
before my eyes go *crazy,* please

seep this night from my grasp. Make
it spin, make it
last;
void, I beg you, take me.
Soul, I beg you, rape me,
and make my dreams much, much
too fast.

I could murder the light inside us all.
        Slaughter me,
                vanquish me, quick!

*Telescreen fuzz vomits names like: gender, and morality. I do not recognize. How much **GRIT** does a mind need to capture, in order to be "human **kind**?" A place where space is equivocal, and days aren't numbered by sun loops, but our own... Oh, I can dream. I can fantasize.*

Witch God;

I was a fire,
combusting to dance and
fuck the air.

I breathed like smoke,
bellowing grey stench,
and oak.

I was an ember,
glowing just to glow,
and going places no one ever
dares to know.

Then just like that,
I'm sober...
Unsatisfied and ignored.
Why can't I be normal
in a bell curve of faith,
dauber?
I'd rather be blind,
and dull,
than burning alive.
Of the fantasies that bored
their way into my mind,
yours, and your hope,
are the cheapest of lies.

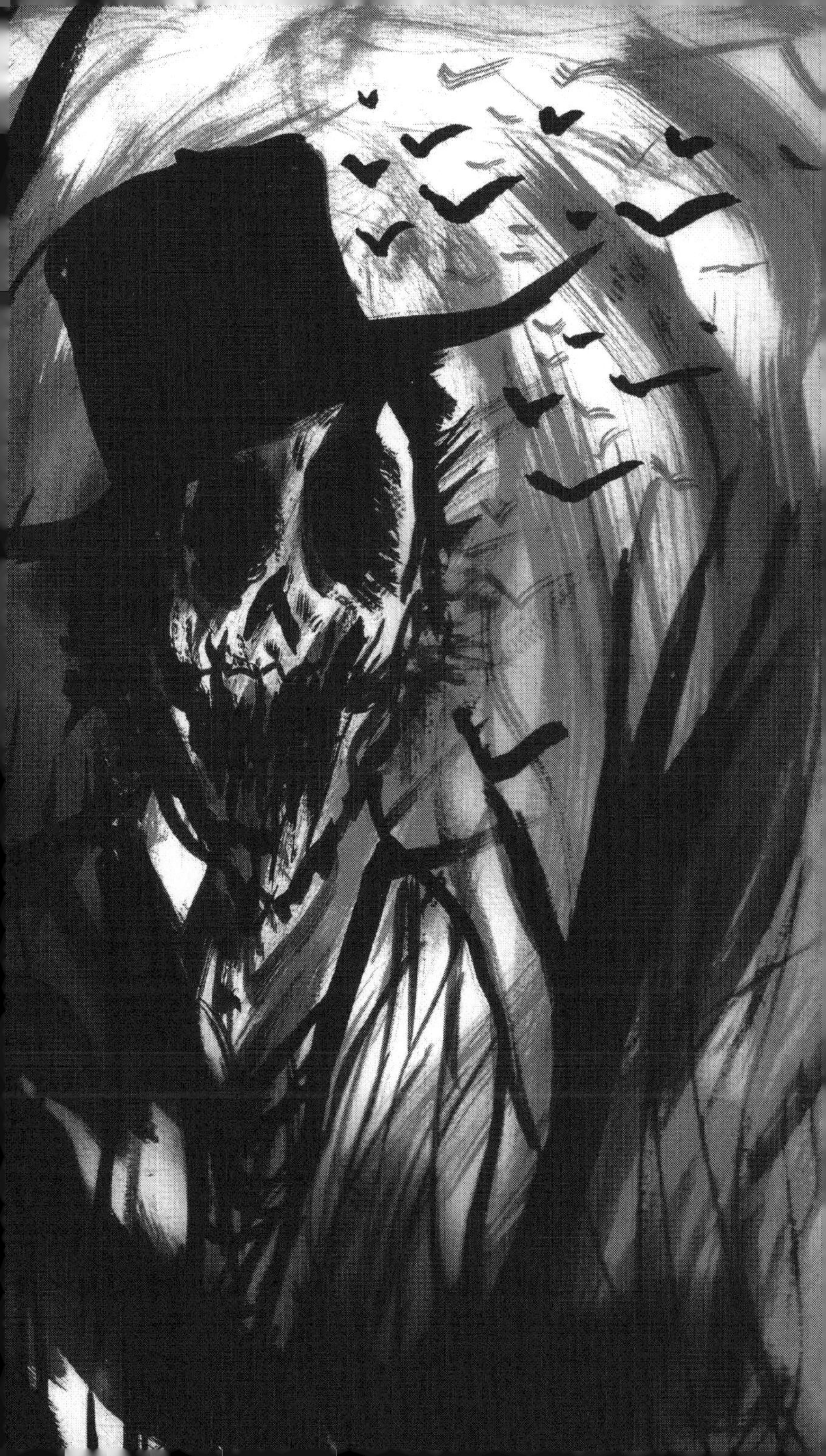

Opal;

You left me on the rocks,
        now I distill
                in a world chaste,
        dull, and slewed.
How the rays beat down on the thirst
                      of my Earthly night.
How I will *NEVER **SATISFY***,
but stumble to my knees,
begging the last drops to sink. sink. into me.

        All my filth caught on a leap,
                to battle my shadow, and sink.
        Sink into the shore of siren howls.
                Of shimmering stones.
                      Of freedom
                      to know
                      and be known.

All is Fair in a World on Fire;

Nurse me back to hell;
to believe in that poison...
I think I've been poisoned...
The whole strip in my blood,
it kills all I've wandered.

I dreamt once... one time I swore
I would change this world.
You could've came with, but now,
I think

We seek best when we're holstered
in our beds, so very, very safe away...

Whatever my wind shows, well,
you'll hear me then.
Hymns of dreams so dead... so thin...
...and that's where I'm heading.

So I'll ask myself,
   are you okay?
  Because I'm either too pitched to let it sink
in, or too sane to ever
      hear it.

So I guess I'll keep suffering the singe and twines
of guilt, after you wrap them over your own
unknown flesh.
     Maybe one of us will make it
out
  unscathed.

To Die;

Teeth
        like gates to Hell;
I am Sisyphus. A leaking cork of wine
        on tongues of Cerberus.
A dirty rotten mirror of
        casual…

        Reflect the code of snakes and tails,
          eating snakes and tails,
          eating skies of hail, while
          rails of white
          bite
          nostril snails and

<u>*I am but consumption*</u> –

I am casual.
    use me.
        Tie me up and casually abuse me.
Tell me I'm a whore,
    a sin,
        a mistake you'll never *make again.*
    Lick my ears with lustful tales of how you'll DIS-APP-EAR
    like robot fads and children's fears
I AM JUST. <u>*SO*</u> ~~<u>*CASUAL*</u>~~.

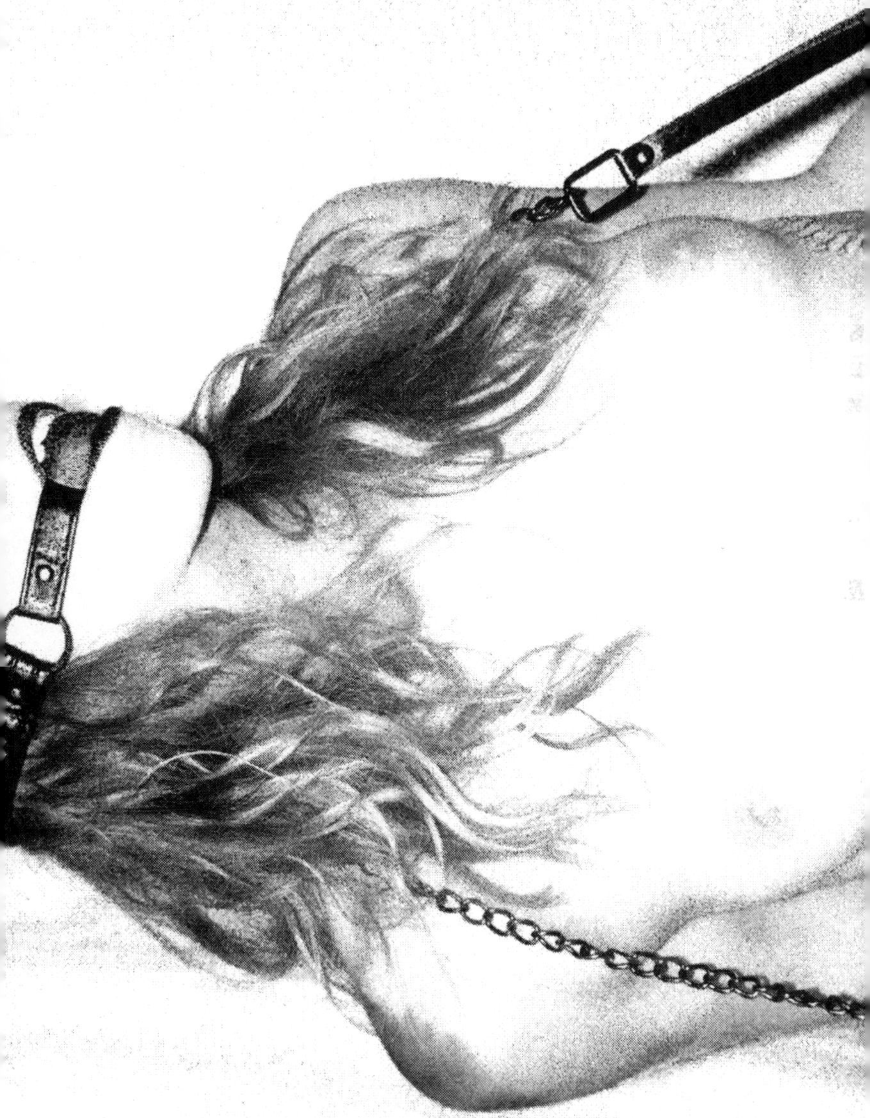

WE HARBOR THE MONSTERS WE CONQUER, UNTIL WE SEE THEM OFF AGAIN.

**WHO YOU ARE,
DEPENDS ON WHAT YOU DO
WITH YOUR HURT.**

Dead Stars Shine for You;

… a precious harmony;
you loved the ones that
meant the most; the
ghosts of mildewed memory.

Somehow, tonight,
the stars burn with more color than
afore.
Somehow
that might mean something…

It's okay to be in the places
you are now. I promise
it still means something,
maybe more,
that I never have to be
a mildewed ghost of nights
afore.

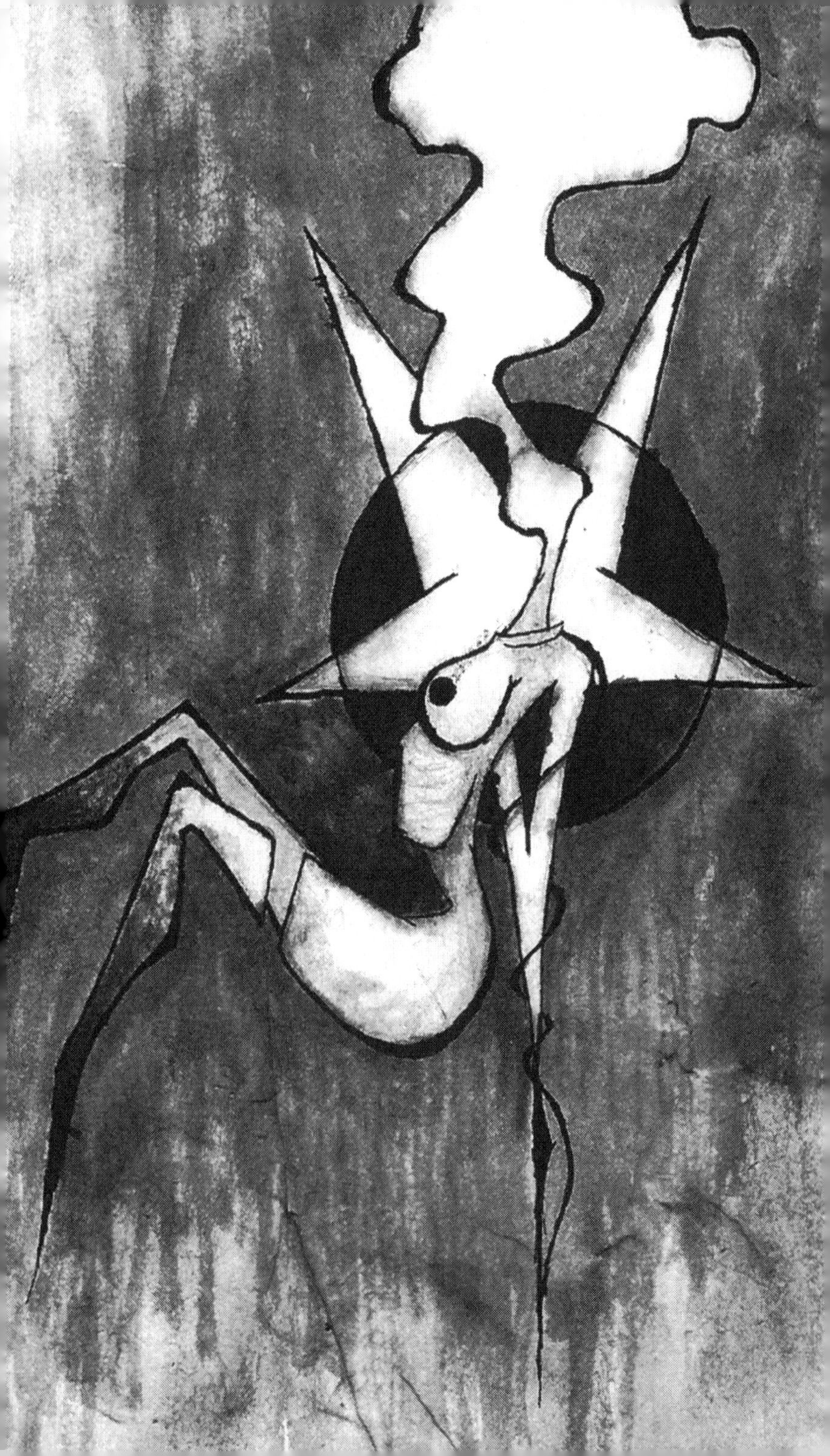

I Want to Fuck God;

God, I'm such a whore.
Just like everyone else,
I'm nothing more than a
fucking toy
      doll;
        smile at me please,
            don't stop smiling
                at your pit –
– your tool, to drool and
         use to cum
     then quit.
I'm nothing special, just
             a filthy
        dream and drug.
Just like everybody else.
Such a whore.

        oh, me? Me?! *I'M* the *whore?*
Please,
    please, she said
*you're **just** as bad as me... you play your game of wit and drench my mind with spit... and I lick your soul like you lick my clit, because that's what we do. Right? That's what we DO! **WE PLAY** with each other. **WE COVER OUR PAIN IN LAUGHS AND KINKS AND IM SO AFRIAD TO BE YOUR LOVER.** You're just as bad as me...*

Secretions of the Beast

She said, you're just as bad as me... but there's a
difference, damn it. There's a difference
                                         because,
I would never do to them what you made me see.

I watched you go.
And go.
And go so ever slowly.

I watched you fade like a false memory...
        but the biggest difference here is that
I would've given myself to you.
You said we're just as bad as one another, we're
both the equal whore; well guess what?
I would've given myself to you...

I don't want to always be this faucet leak of gore
erotica.
I wanted to be yours.
I wanted to be yours.
I want to fuck God; mother nature can have her
way with me.
Satan can chew my thighs and bring
righteous tear drops to my eyes;
I'd fuck Kronos 'till the end of time,
and Saturn in the same night.
I'd cum inside of Jesus Christ,
and suck Brahman off his holy crest.
I want
        to fuck
                God
        and you were the closest to her that I ever
        came.

Mule;

It wasn't afraid to give its name.
By imitation of beloved strain and body,
it fermented into my ultraviolet night.
An attendance felt by sobs so soft,
and relentless shakes;
a power recognized in flickering...
The demon knows just what it takes to
bring you near its dream.
At first, you'll hear its sorrow pain,
and agonizing misery;
but as it slowly finds its grasp
you'll only hear its snickering.

The name you've given has been cursed; the name
you've begged to aid.
the ways you've calmed has been rehearsed in its
new serenade and
it throws you over!
        It slams you under!
                It captures your control...
This opioid Demon
pale
with eyes as bright as gold;
with eyes that rest in blackest clouds
it's face begins to sharpen.
Behind cheeks like beetle teeth and brows of antler
roots, the mouth is wide and ready
to chew,
      chew,
           chew you open.

Leaving;

I was your son,
        but your still alive,
                like a needle made of history, you're
still a thorn in my minds side, and
        I want you to know,
                      by God, mom
                              I tried –

I tried to be every holy blessing you ever prayed
for; I tried to be the freshest apple of your eyes…
I begged to know you like I wish you'd have known
me – I starved
to be the biggest heart our hell could hide,
        and
God dammit mom, I swear
        on the bible that you still hold close
        to your heart,
on the scriptures you still fetishize,
        and on the holy union that tore us apart,
            the pantheon romanticized,
I swear to *GOD I TRIED* –

        but to you, and all I knew,
        I died.

It isn't right that a bond as old as time or longer,
could be broken by a few missteps. It
isn't right that I'm no stronger than the stones
they place on top of graves – I want to **FEEL**! To

feel the tenderness of something real, something
true, and of that feeling mom, I relied in you…

Secretions of the Beast

So,
Why am I so hard to look at in the mirror? Not of light but time –
why is my reflection not the right one?
Why am I so ALONE
      even with MYSELF – WHY
WONT
you
FORGIVE ME?

Because I swear I know, that you think it wasn't you, but

    Why'd the FUCK did you HAVE to HIT ME?!
                      And sure...
We'll say I barely bled, but,
        what heaven did you give me?
When the God you serve is Hell or worse;
When your mother says your dead to her;
I swear... to God... I tried.

So when I said, "I love you too,"
        which one of us had lied?

SLUT;

So clear, I'll keep my mind, amidst madness.
    Against borrows of worms
and electrical strain.
    To remain afloat in blackness,
    dreamed
Eden's cane,
    *a world of **meaning**...*

Can I be the bloodletting of your
brightest lamb?
Can I be your bread and wine?
A volt of purpose; death symbolized;
Can I identify with this
blackest mass?
Hike, to pull, and yank me
up Satan's mountain;
Lucifer's cane.
Cripple my fountain of faith,
and execute my pain in gallows
and rum
and gauze.
Kill my Gold. Oil. Drugs.
Kill,
my G.O.D.
Kill.

Thrown through your thoughts breathing

Don't Go;

Can't feel your hands as
        my hands anymore;
all I feel
    is regret.
So, did she as well?
        I'm left to beg,
            please God no...
like a diamond,
    hanging around,
        she climbed above the king and
crown...
Even when you stalk the darkness
of what's "done to be done,"
...I'll be there...
    There is no muse of
        Tomorrow.

So,
    if I killed myself tonight;
I'll be there.

Climb up your crown.

Foreplay;

I'm nothing but a pen, my dear.
What was or should be expected of this,
is far too delicate for
ink on paper.
I am not a human soul,
entrenched in skin,
or luck, to be yanked and hung to dry,
like a charm.
I am not yours. I am not yours.

I am not my own.

I am but a pen, my dear.
Kill me so that I may live forever.
One way or another, lover,
I never have to die.
Kill me, damn it, fuck me dead;
I see heaven in those eyes.
Angels creep inside my head,
peering souls immortalize…
Kill me, drain me, make me red;
I need the heaven
in your
eyes.

Secretions of the Beast

Rum;

Don't let these halos sharpen your eyes, or the ails of the Leyak tickle your spine. The sludge of the morning will clear you the lesson of luck; or you may be consumed by the night. Once more into the abyss, on the rocks, slightly shaken.
Thrice forward and taken outside of you
to forget
       to forget
              to black out and split apart by every fiber you've left through history.
     I'm scared of you, and what you're capable
              of.

Property;

Her dirty thighs are thick, and pulsing
mystery, seeding grit and grain
under my heart.
I don't want to hurt you; I want
to let this go,
but
the shock of my groin
when my brain paints your pain
around my lips – oh God Devil whore
        I cannot stop this…

I feel a boil in my blood,
with this soft cunt wrapped around my mind;
I feel a feeling that we had
but
        no longer care to find; my love,
my sweetest dream, my dove,
I cannot say I'm blind to all
these sins of lust.

My agonizing angel, do not
search to see my soul.
I cusp my breath into your ear
and pray you will not know of me.
        For it is me.
This underlying prying sin, for it is me
who enters in and takes her;
    fucks her;
        consumes her;
            destroys her;
                ravages her;

dooms her...
for she is next to face this sexual
                           choking
                                   vine.
For when she falls in love,
        I'll be back to change her mind.

Oh how I love the sight of my soul,
        ultimately our soul
in
        the collection of this life.
As if a beetle tolls the road it takes,
                as if the bristles scream the
picture I paint;
        so too does life fold and turn unto itself.

We belong to no one, and so,
                I'll always be around.

Secretions of the Beast

Be Nothing;

You are but nothing to me.
A casualty of my loathing,
livid in a bore.
There are imprints of ropes, and
insecurity,
and my room still smells like whore.
I
don't want to sleep on bitter sheets
of filthy residue.
I
have eyes that watch without a mouth,
and lips that meet only after I'm inside.
I have words that reflect a madness; a
nightmare plague we strive to hide.
You
are not like me, and I
am far from you.
                      I am not like you.

Still, I play your tortured role
of needy little pest.
I play it with every flower crave,
and save this role
to rest.
Aloof, uncaring, how dare you fall for me.
Please, I need you, I'm never this happy.

      and so we're all around, just waiting
                to be plucked.
Flowers
      begging bee's
             and willows, to see

they're worth a fuck to give
outside of honey dreams.
> To drizzle sugar and lick the cum
> > off kings and queens.

That all our hopes come true, beg;
that all our hopes come true,
> in the midst of this great haze;
"all things come to those who wait,"
> they chant in endless craze...

> Maybe hopes are always meant to just be
hopes? To drown and never surface through...
> Maybe we are that much alike,

> > for I am but nothing to you.

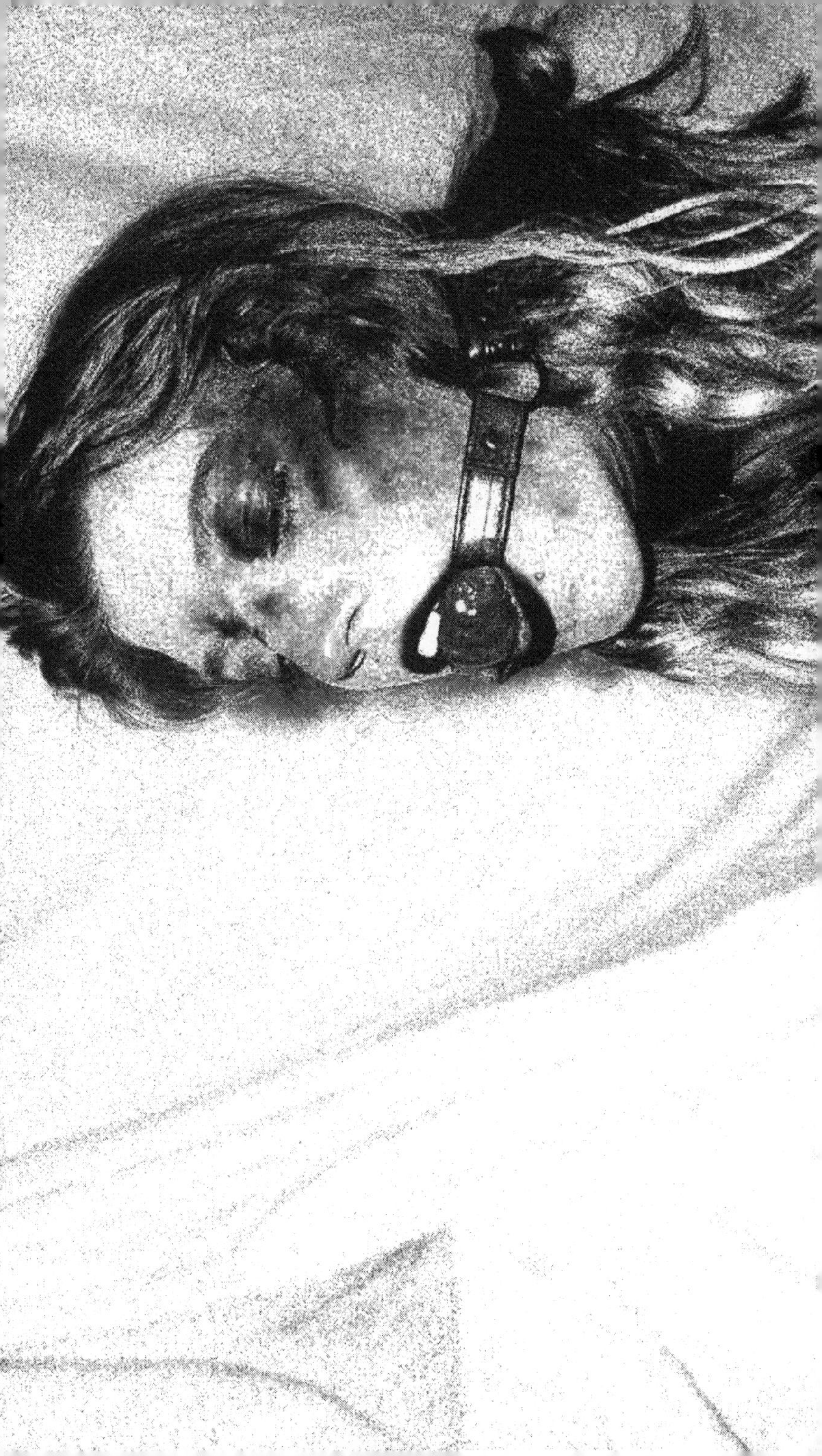

Tulips;

Roll your eyes; roll your eye.
Roll your pretty little die.
                        die.
                       die
                                      in my direction.
Fill my holes and tongue and nose with your
infection, and spill your luck all over me.
Your mind
          is like a cherry I can chew; just
                    be wary of the pit.
You're this flame
          without a breath, and
                    Percy Sherry counterfeit;
                            and oh, how they want
                                        you;
these blind and zombified;
                    these lonely horrified…
Oh, how you lead the maggots in your tongue – the
tongue I used to kiss.
          See how you give yourself to every
little nothing missed?
You disgusting, stupid, nothing *gift,* I resent the
very light we once shared between our
iris's, above a moon full of water, beneath the
reflection of Venus.
          So I cannot be me absolutely, not
without the ember I harbor bursting to full flame.
I   miss   being able to
    hate   you.

Finch;

It feels like robbery; the thing that steals itself.
From friends,
family,
beloved, beloved…

It feels like desperate silence,
deafening and merciless.
Chaos, so still, like a star; and see?
How they shine for you…

It feels like I've been stolen from myself.
Then, not just me, but everyone else,
and I am unwanted by either.

It feels like I could fly away, and that could be just fine.

Association;

No, you're my favorite kind of sinner.
The kind with rafters in your eyes; the kind
that lives because of genocide.
It rattles in your mouth,
the sistrum you suck off each night, on bruised
and bloodied knees. It's just another whore
for you to worship – your own tail of programmed
moral righteousness. Your own heart you plead to please
with backwards broken law. You're my favorite
sinner, because you're the closest thing I've seen to raw.
Raw, yes, RAW when you spite those

                    who wear clothes
              you were brain washed to
hate.
Raw when you refuse to eat food
            from the hands of a FAG and

RAW when I slam
      my hardon in your ass
              because it's technically not
                  premarital sex.

Oh, yes, my pretty perfect *sinneréss*, pray.
      Get on your knees and pray, you closet
racist pervert chimp.
          Your worship tastes so good when
it's dripping in confusion.
It's funny how the hooker is in hell, and I've just
somehow shown you heaven for free.

It's funny how your god will never forget about me.

HalleluyelyaH;

You're a stranger, soul,
and what our eyes know is
but a courageous roll of vanishing.
Thinner, farther, the distant voice scratches in a
yearn *PUSH!*
   PUSH THE BOUNDARIES!
FOR YOU MAY FEEL ONE
    GOD
   DAMN
     THING!

Oh,
  Stranger soul;
    damaged, damaged dream.
How unfair a life, so the life you seem to be,
for here for me,
for *one goddamn **thing***.
It tries and tries again,
this piss poor insanity.

I saw you before you did.

A March on Morality;

Porcelain angel,
brittle and wet in the muck of still
water;
melted in a mirror of God.
God.
Of GOD to pray
for something,
oh, my lord, anything more.

    Ah, we're walking on grass like red dew covered knives, green and shimmering in the misty memory between good and what's left.
Remember when we were children, doe? When being naked meant nothing more than the absence of clothes, and now our fur is dripping in sweet pheromone aroma. Our hooves are hallowed, hard and confident. Our tails are open wide.

    Remember when we couldn't wait to get inside, and ride the walls of wet, warm heaven? *The last of us*, the children sing, *the last of us will splash among this venom drop of milky cum. A final song fulfilling notes that wrap around our tongue.*

    Capture caterpillars and squeeze them inside out. Throw your dirt around my name and dig me deeper in the fields, the woods, the rivers we explored before our bodies.

I'm perfectly hollowed, the children say, *I'm perfectly allowed to hate you. For you stranded me here, alone and unaware of how to counteract the horrors you couldn't help but fuck. Yes,* **fuck***,* they scream, *you* ***fucked*** *these horrors into our lives. You spewed your angry dogma and naked fleshy needs. You begged to be. You **BEGGED to BE** and built machine, machine, hypnotized by whore and war and more machines.*

*So we too will **FUCK** and **DRINK** and **DIE to DIE** because it's all that's left. So we too will imbibe the breath of **SIN** and **LUST** and give ourselves to your God,*

and in a pause, they raise their grass up to their pale, button nose, to sip red tear drops from their eyes,

Your god is death.

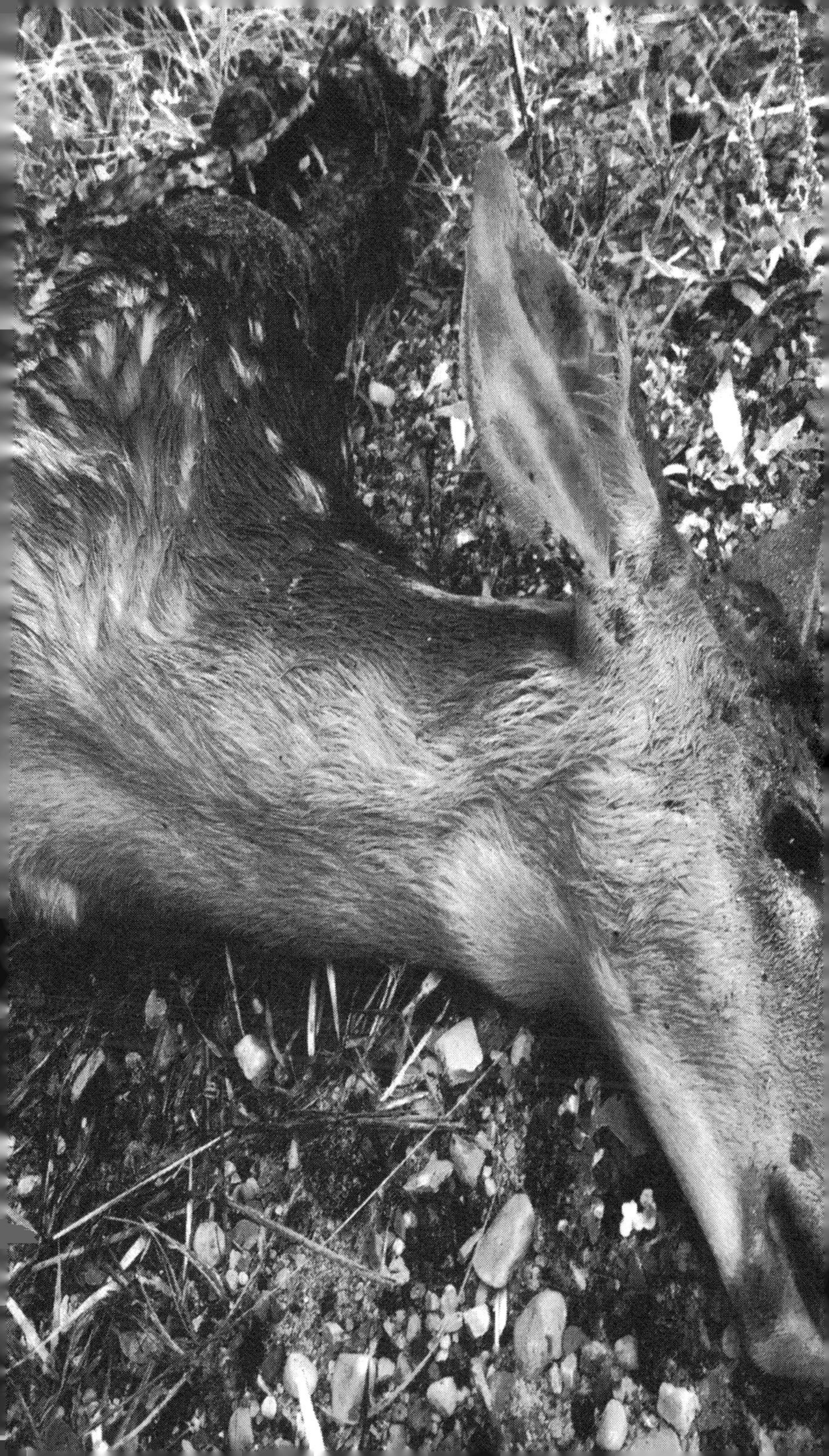

-My dear angel, your Devil;

Were you thinking of me?
What more could a beggar implore than a release
of his inquiries...
What monster, where-out eyes invariably spill
forth disaster...
Of my garments,
      my accessories governed to me by
Adramelech himself...
Were you thinking of me, or my words;
my being, or the blood that I paint with?

Because I've fixated on you, my rodent queen.
      I see your songs,
the notes you swirled around my tongue,
            and the photographs you burnt into
my silver dish.
I see you in too much these days, and it only ever
makes me wish for lakes, pines, and log cabins.
For sharp axes,
        and roaring fires,
               with smores and soaked
               shoes.
Maybe the dripping of a skinned doe,
        and dried bones, burnished and
sapient.
Of you, my vellum soul; my dear angel.
It makes me wish of you.

Conversion;

I always told her that I was a dæmon.
One day, instead of just laughing, she told me to prove it... so I did.

It was six months before she asked to see me again, and as we sipped our coffee, she told me to "*say it*, the way you always did before, just this time *once more*."

        So, I kissed her.
Because some things can't be said with words, and only bodies open doors.
        We were never meant to be, like
Autumn never touches Summer it was a script of nature... but we were never the type to do things by the book.
We were rebels without a cause. I was the cut, and she was the gauze.
        Where every **BREATH** that we took was given to one another as ammunition, to tear down the others inert and holy mission but

    I   didn't   care.

I was too busy
commanding my fingers to swim laps through her hair... and wishing that I had mind control, so that her lips could split and smile every time that I stare.
She was order,

and I was chaos.
I wore black, and she wore a cross.
               Where not only did its silver
radiance attempt,
to no prevail, to sail a storm of God's righteous
hail, to end and oppose my pentagram; it acted
to demonstrate a simple diagram, that the paths of
our ventricular
was always meant to be perpendicular.
Touching merely once,
for an intoxicating,
               euphoriant,
                           infuriating holy moment.
Touching just once,
      eternally locked in one spherical frame of
the pasts domain, to dilute and fall forever
backwards...

Touching at all, was all we really needed to fill up
one another's pots of the seeded thoughts we
secreted into our lives of water;
      we grew until we could extinguish the
flames that ailed our history.

She was less than an echo,
               leaving more of a print than a stain
does, but a stain
               is all she'll ever be.

Angels, and Demons,
they keep us separated, her and me.

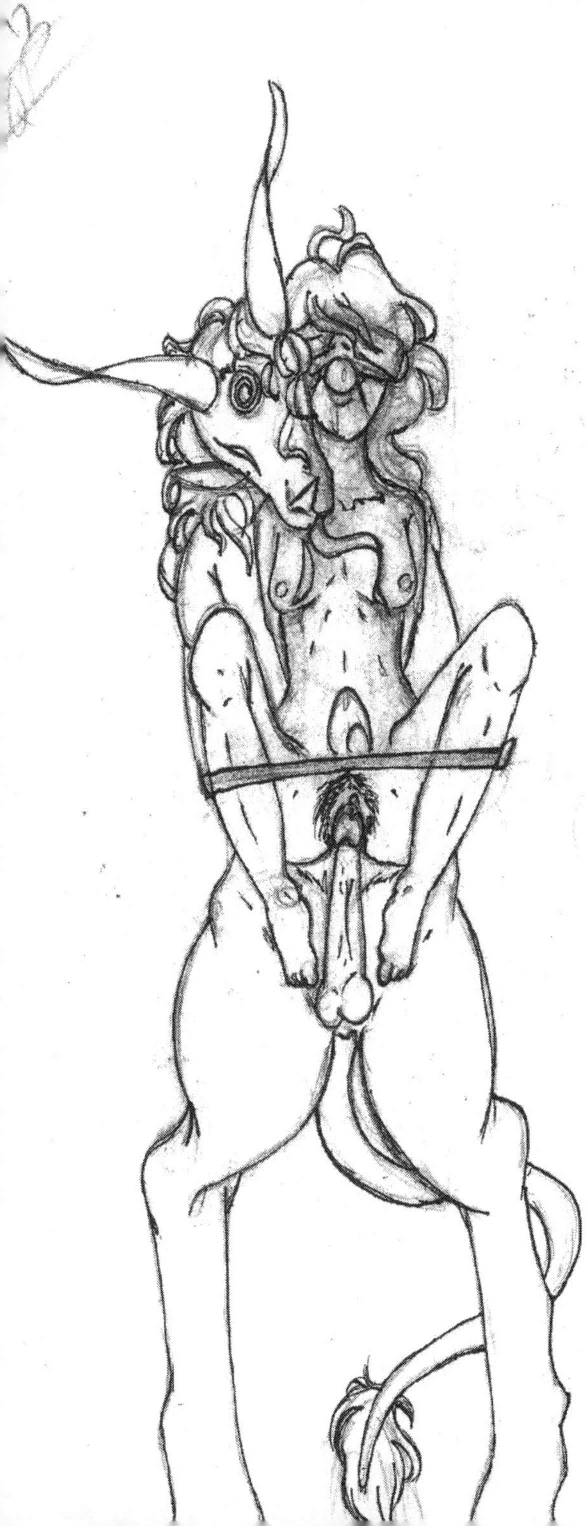

Broken Hour;

Home
in the iris of the black hole I behold,
burning the event horizon on my chest.
Cease fire of the ticking sands,
so we may drool them over, and fall back again.

We are unfazed, my breath and my lungs, by the culture of this human race.
We sit in this parking lot until I am dawn.
Until I see the violet lips, and pristinely white eyes.
Until I recognize the mother from beyond our ether.
Until I feel the perpetual pull, the gravity in our souls; an attraction to stars
will always leave us burnt.
No longer do I look at the lights where it shines,
but instead the blackness left blind,
to wind and bend the light around our
eating pupils.
Unless we beg to never be satisfied,
we will always have an end.
Unless we rule the numbness of nirvana,
we will always have an end.

Lineage and phlogiston;

Red flags stay white, until the blood has dried,

and like a list, I wore your past.

The urge to scream the scars you hide,
from very first, to last.

I wasn't meant for hearing sighs,
or long-lasting autumn nights,
whose fire logs burn slow with comfort,
extinguishing my lonely name.

We inherit them, and all their trauma flames;
half their light is in our own,
hidden, smeared and encrypted in
decisions, behavior, lust, and horrors.

The bringers of death, the genesis of determined
casualties. God is a pig, eating its young.
My, are they always so hungry; the swine that
grow our lives.
Perpetual harvests left defeated seeds, and now no
flower bothers with spring.
Every hint of affection signals red, red flags.

Traumas stay neutral until white curtains fall,

and like a script I mark my flesh.

My bones implore I confess your sins, until the
crop you've grown, has bloomed.

China White;

I am the tar you created.
The hate in the sex,
and bore of beginnings.
I'll be the death that you love
for every drug you hate it for.
The capsule of nowhere, to practice the hex
of spawning a whore.
The growth of a game you'll lose
when I become adhesive.
Black boiling goo to burn you to your bones.
Obsidian reflections bounce between this
sacrifice poltergeist;
you've made me flame and magma.
You'll love me now, won't you?
When you learn to scry the expansions
of my marble skin?
Oh God I must be insane;
I must be unhinged.
By the powers invested in me, Demon,
What is your name?
By the Dark Lord and hallow syringe,
I shall vanquish you.
What is your name?!
Satan will always leak through my veins,
in the most pleasurable of ways,
but as for you, lore;
addicting, insatiable, chemical gore;
I've beaten your game.

9-21-2016;

On this day, I met a bug.

You ever notice the days that have the bluest skies? The days where all you want is to be outside
to soak it up in every sense of sight and touch?
I never seem to miss those days, and yet, by God, I almost missed her when she walked by.
She was a day whose bluest skies beaming smile could tangle time and make you question, "What was I worrying about just now?"
She was a day whose sunniest oceans and palest sands would never cease to roll and dance warm memories into our beaches.
She was a noon whose hours would tie together yesteryears of every pivotal point; of awkward memories, and painful sorrows; of every single breath you've took – yes! This is what it's all led up to...

I'd never dreamed a day as rich with potent passion as her, and yet there she stood,
Right in front of this daze of mine, just laughing a laugh that I know, without a doubt, has saved a hundred lives...
It certainly saved mine.
Have you ever wished that you could smell the night sky? I watched it sing around her movement, in synch with her own dance of vital life, as strands on strands wisped their way onto her shoulders. A kind of darkness that invites you

in, when you're exhausted from your endless shift, and worn out eyes just beg to be set to slumber.

God, she was a life. Not just a passerby, but a life of a thousand lives all wrapped into one eye, and at this place I found myself so tranced in thought,
    in awe,
        in infinity I'd almost missed her this time...
As though her feather skin hadn't radiated among the dullness of the room around us.
As though her voice couldn't seduce even the flowers to bend their heads her way. As though I
Was a fool, full of sorrow, and amazement, that if I weren't to do something soon I'd never see this girl again.
So when I say she was a day I'd never had before, and when I say she was a night I'd always ever dreamed of, I can't even begin to describe how all of heaven must've lent their ear to hear our conversation.

You exist in a world where she never said yes, or no. You may never know the way my voice had tremored and shook, or stood proud at attention, just grateful to give itself to her. You'll never know of our lives afterward of a yes, and no.
here is authentic validation that this moment was never overlooked. This graceful scene that'll never go away, regardless of if it carried through, will always be imprinted now in time and space and a dimension above, inside me and you, because.... she's worth that.

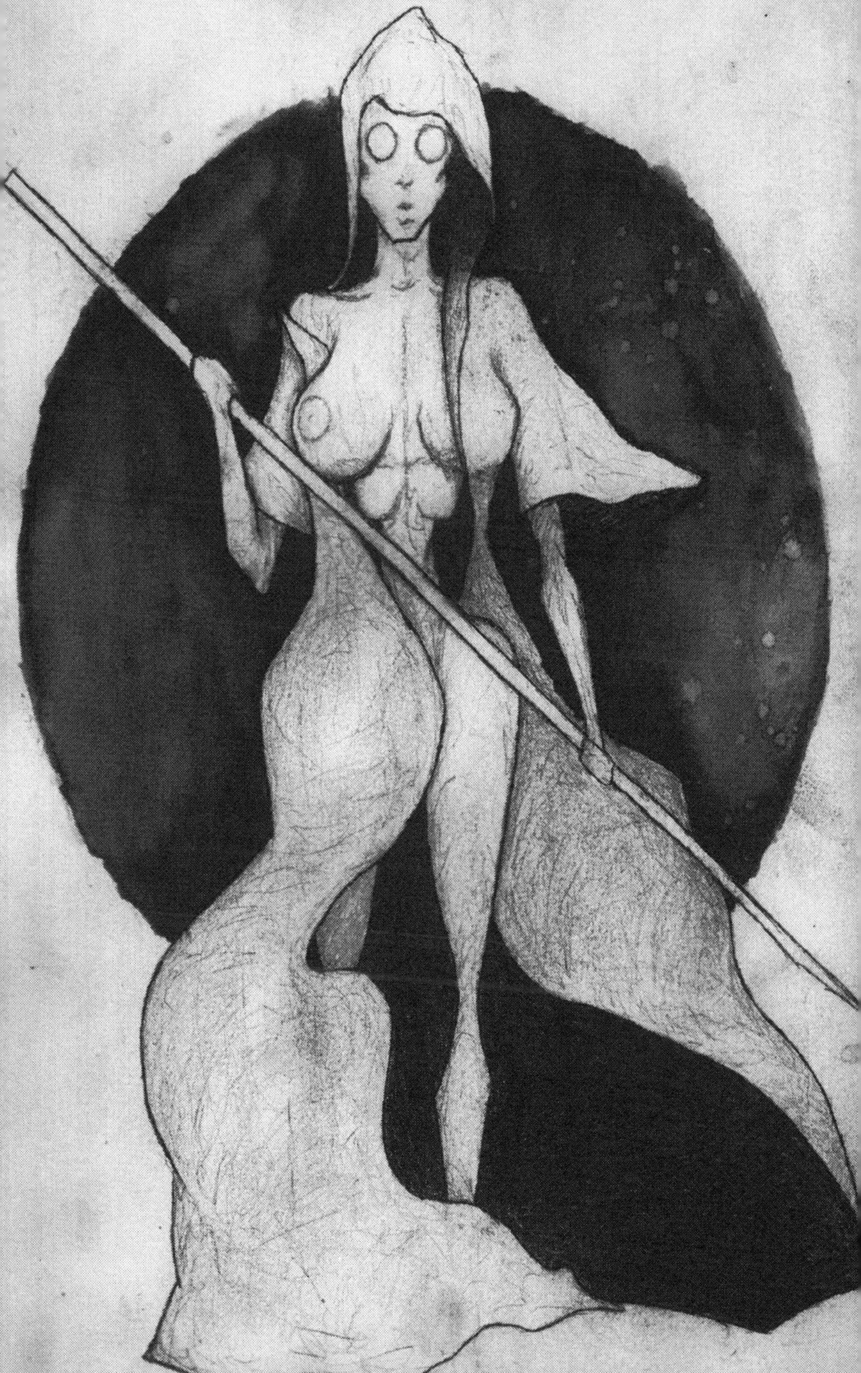

Alp;

Generation slumber;
    an age without numbers
        or reason
            for answer.
Just open ended
    alpha waves and identity.
A Satanic source of creativity.
So it came to me, this queercubus;
this ghost of dead egos,
    and with its serpent tongue it
entered through the nasolacrimal.

        It melted from a plaster door and perched
            away from my delusion.
Hypnotic yellow iris pairs bore heavy waves of
insecurity.
        I was doomed to be this nightmare
mist by modern medicine,
    just like it was doomed to possess me.

Cry blood from the nipples of mother woes, and
permeate my Evil Eye.
            Feed on me, with talon teeth,
                and banana cherry
                spit.

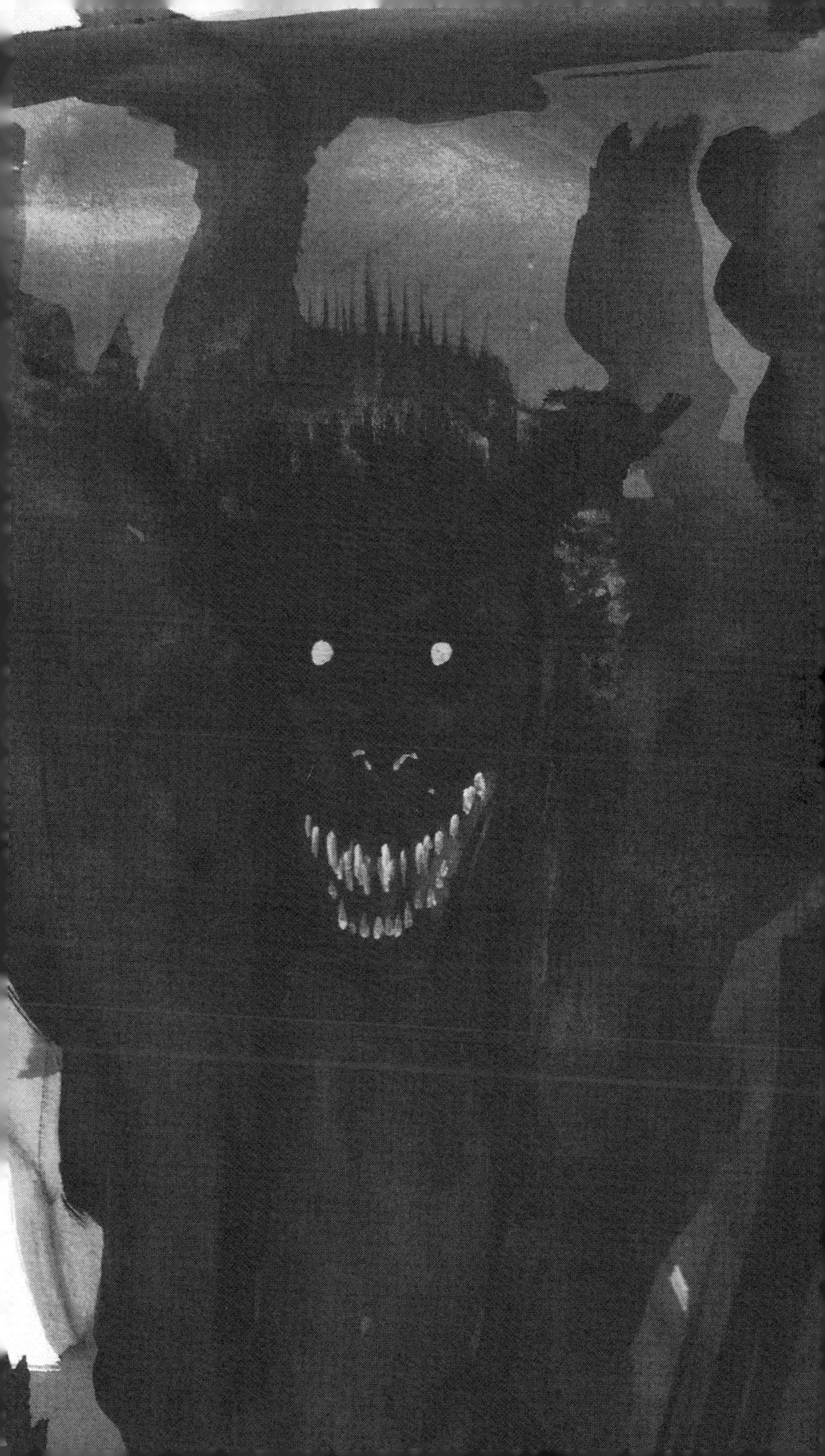

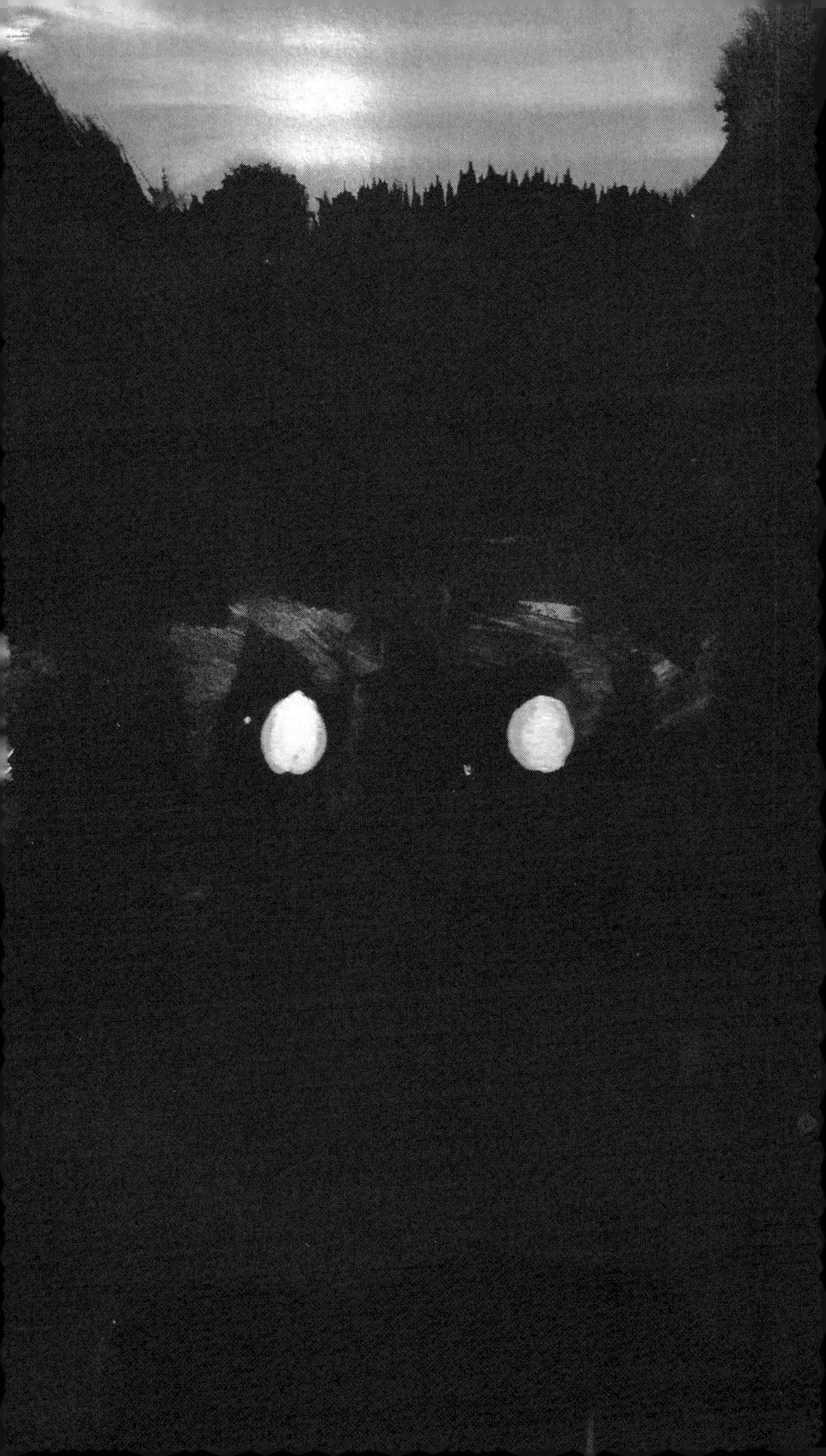

Coy Pond;

Now you will show me how to live like grace,
and I will do this
    on my next dying day.
Within the intrinsic system of my blood core,
        the coy of Styx swim in secrets.
How could I ever fall away
                from you?
You taught me how to live
    and suspend above a lake of
        scrutiny.
In this passing
you showed me to capricious
                love.

                The sparrows and Benu
              roll above indigo skies,
                  just out of reach
                from my ever ending,
                    autopilot,
                  vantage point.

        I would only ever be a fool
            if I never
            begrudgingly
            thanked you.

The hybrid burn
and soothe;
illuminate
and blind.

The sun.

Treaty;

I was plastered here because, I don't know why.
Does everything have to be so structured?
So compartmentalized...
Do I even need a name to exist in this space?
I'm stuck; as still as broken skulls.
Will the pines of uncertainty infest the message, if I'm without a face?
Can I just say what I want to
                            feel to
                                         need to say?
See I don't think so...
Not with *these* eyes.
        Not with these caterpillar bugs crawling
                to inch
their way towards me, and chew invariably on their own lies...

        you're on a mission, you know... to show the world that you're not like *it*;
                and don't you hate *it*?
                        Don't you hate every last little *bit*?
Why enjoy the peaks from the valley? Why consume like Nazareth?
So, could I play this antithesis; this **Set**, this **Satan Lucifer**? Could I play this thing that you are horribly afraid of?
A devil's advocate;
        A cross † reference;
                A carnal unleashing;
                        A ***raw*** power;

or is it just doing my best to be…
        I'm not attacking you, I swear.
I'm not attacking anybody here,
                        Or there…
I just wish to be…
I just. Wish. To be.

*I love you. Doesn't that **matter**?*
I love you; not the feeling but the act…
See words are a lot to demons like me but action spells will always spill forth more into reality.
See? I love you.
I don't know why that doesn't matter…

Now I can't feel my teeth, I'm leaning
on a serenade. I can't feel
the meat I'm chewing on this last crusade;
and I *have* life; I **have** the meaning; I don't have a brain.
I have tales of songs to forfeit, but I don't know my name.

So, I'll <u>live</u> on this carousal of violence,
        I'll love like a lost grenade.
I'll love like it's all that's left, the silence of the serenade.

I have all the stories haunted; I have all the lore.
I have everything I wanted but I am *JUST* a whore…

I have learned to live unlasting, wanting nevermore... I don't know what I forget... I don't know what I've forgotten.

ϕ

All we know are the blood
       and the bones,
              and the hieroglyphs of the *catacombs. All we know are the tombs of the low,*
that the time to atone is the time to atone.

Embers rise to the sky. I don't have love. I don't have reason to see that I'm living to die, and I don't have highs. The lows in my eyes say the treason is living in lies. But...

    *All we know are the *blood* and the bones, and the hieroglyphs of the catacombs. All we know are the tombs of the low,*
    *that the **time** to atone*
        is
    *the time to **atone**.*

Sheep;

Convicted by the hurt of countless bleats, like thorns of a hypnotized rose, or the rivers of red that drain my heartless dreams. It's as if this world is as cold as it calculates, and the bones of the Nephilim congregate in concrete dogma, and the endless souls we trample as a day to day commodity bear it like a mission.

I'm only as lucid as need be because I'm not really here; none of it is happening. It's of that, I hurt the most. When the parameters of our body become the lateral scene of a hazy sphere we dream 'perception,' and of a sphere of spheres we call out 'Demiurge!'

It eats us all abound with the appetite of Cronus; with the stomach of time, war, and indifference. It's as if "history repeats itself, first in tragedy, second in farce." Yet what just reality should let I dance the words of a racist, anti-Semitic fraud like Karl Marx?

What poet of cult following should I parrot like a prophet, and of the rounded 4,200 faiths, which one shall my tongue hold?

Tongue and teeth and cheeks like spears and canon barrels and saliva as consistent as blood and blood and blood and time. Which dialectic of frame and mind shall overrun my life? It's as if we're only as free as we allow ourselves to be, and of this future freedom one must always fight the acid sheets of myopia.

Do not follow me, ever. Not me or anyone or anything; there's nowhere to go anyway.

Please;

I feel broken, like I'm not meant to remember, yet how dare I forget.
Though everything sings, it feels
                                    so far away.
                  Every time you answered my
echo, with a force of nature so true, it rescued me the soothing play;
every time it learns to be deficient.

So my heart remembers you, implicitly, and these phasing seasons pump through my coagulated veins to beg a new amnesia.
So my **brain** *responds*, because you won't, and I lash out again.
So the world is cold and I am drowning in all the frozen things I should've said; I should've screamed; I should've begged; I shouldn't be; I should've bled; and I can't say it now –
                                The thing for
spoken things is dead,
                and carved deep into the gravestone,
"love,
                    DON'T GO."

This night is more shallow than the rest. I'm so tired of endless goodbyes. I'm so tired of endless goodbyes. I'm so tired of endless goodbyes.
I'm so tired and I can't change my mind; and I can't beg or fight or try and try and try. It is not fair. It is not fair. There is no worthy truth to bear of 'right' or 'wrong,' or ready and not. It only hurts.

Micro Tell Inn;

From your failure, love.

You smell like evergreens, elk, and falcon screams.
A tundra cusp, and vision mist as white as light.
With an angel wisp, you make my night
with every maybe "might" of parted portal lips.
Your laugh is like a cabin fire,
        our time is lined in three-fold wire,
                and I can never tire of this vacation
to northern Michigan...

See Baby Bee, you feel like home,
and howling obliteration.
You feel like piano keys
behind time lapsed trees
grown in full erection.

You feel like
the crushing weight of silence, in the alley of a 4
AM blizzard, and instead of going further into that storm,
I sip a whiskey fifth, in leather,
weathered worn,
and pray the day is never born.

Because, I'm just fine in this line of broken glass,
this bed and breakfast overpass,
when any day could be our last,
                        in southern Michigan...

We kiss.

We kiss each other like it's a mission.
At first, we'd barely look each other in the eye, and
now we move without hesitation.
Our world has slowed, our thoughts are racin' –
two pupils of time in
                full dilation.
It's a journey, and battle, with no destination,
but you sing,

                and god how you sing,

of Seattle skies and sea,
of silk white welcomed sheets,
at MicroTell Inn,

and how I dream a legion of sunburnt dreams,
of a day
we visit Washington.

Bathe;

Because I'm supposed to be available.
I'm supposed to belong to
eyes in heads, in eyes;
      observers observed.

I want to talk about the horror;
I want to talk about the universe.
I want to bathe in the notion of a bored design,
      a nothing nightmare,
and puppets strings pulling puppet strings.
I
      don't
            want
                    to drown
                          in something that
      doesn't
            care.

I care.
Too much, I care.
About nothing.

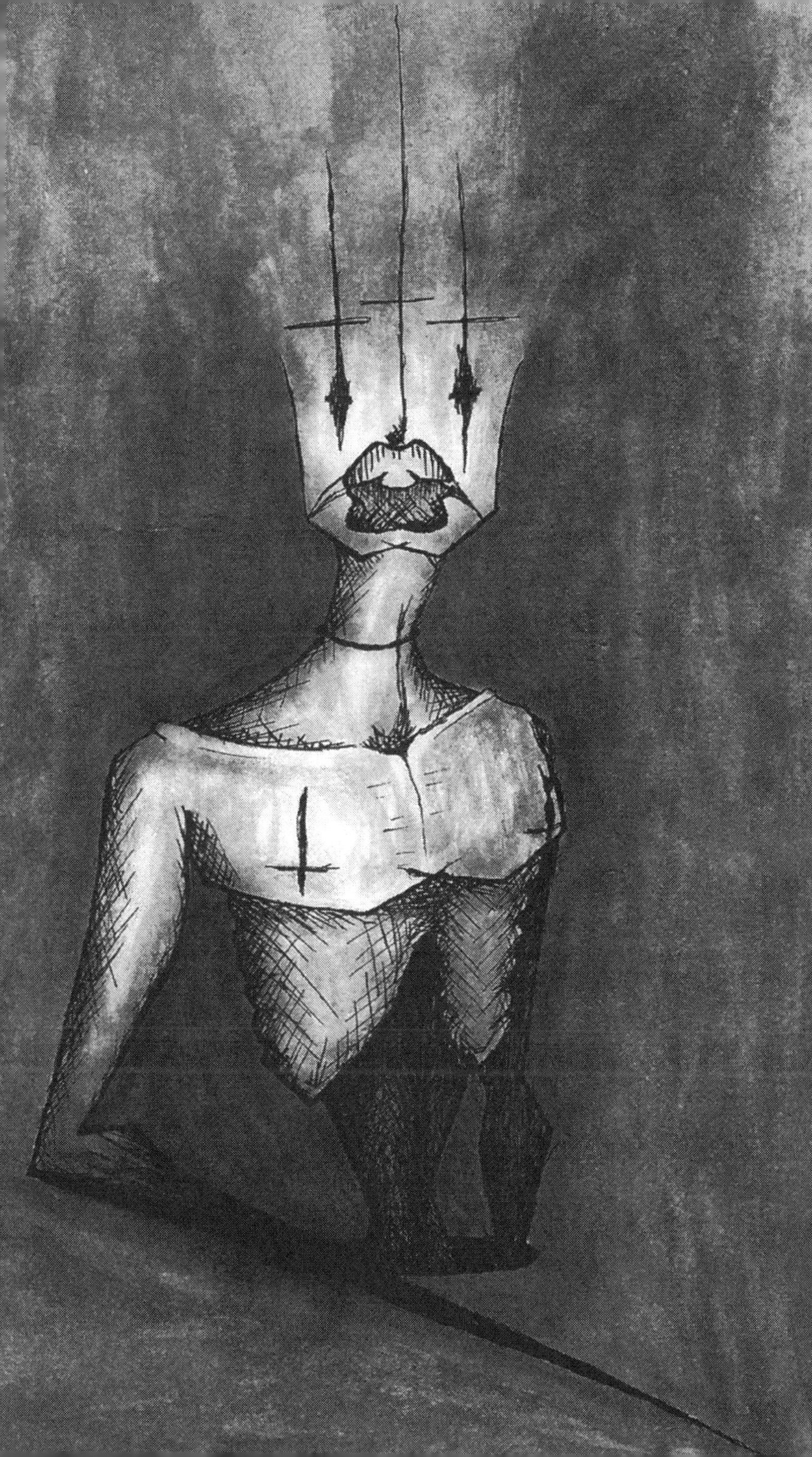

Fizzle Can;

A bee crash lands through carbonation,
and drowns inside Yates cider; I watch with
eyes of oceans, and ponder
as children do.
How many guitar strings did that bee resonate
with? A buzz,
         and a jam,
                        and the trickling smell
    of weed.
    Black lights and lava lamps that scream
I'm plenty sane.
It's you who's crying, not me.
        I muse with the carpet strings
and pillow sheets, while the goldfish sing my safe
words.
    "not me."
                "not me."

Now I'm just fine staring into the liquid
vodka,
    vomit,
        and Japanese Soda.
A mosquito crash lands through carbonation, and
drowns inside philosophy.
    How many times, I wonder, did its needle
vibrate prophecy?
An addict sucks the slate clean again,
           until the mirror shows two little blue
pearls,
        the green inherited by Jerusalem,
and God tells me I've been a bad little boy.

Secretions of the Beast

Please turn your scriptures to the epiphany of love;
they have always left you,
      haven't they?
No, not Him, not God, but they sure do come close.
The beloved,
      the family,
            the smearing of the two.
They have, and always will, crash land away from you.

I stare into the windows of the classroom; all the other kids left me here to die.
I wouldn't die though, for I was far too young, and the bugs had yet to scream their essence of mortality.
Soda and donuts were just soda and donuts, here.
Though I was alone, always.

I watched a chicken hatch from its egg when I was in first grade, and I thought about how long it's been outside of comfort, only to hatch into cold, stale air.

I asked my mom why flowers bothered to bloom each day.
She couldn't answer.

Soft Stage;

This is not the place to miss you; it's the same logic
that beds us in the first place.
Cutting myself shows me I can heal, so,
pull the covers up, my curvy razor blade,
and smooth the lullaby across the way I feel.
We all love to wait to die, and aren't you just a
blessing.
I feel like a lost touch,
 a prayer to pieces,
   a rabbit hole to never know; I feel perfectly
                                                sound
     or whole, and no,

I don't need you, but it makes it easier to breathe
the sunrise in.
I can start today because of last night.
I can continue this endless limbo light
of grey dreams and hopeful amenities.
I can cut myself in half, and make twice as many
enemies.
Brush the teeth of dogs, and shine trotters brand
new.
It's not my place to be the humble thing you
wished would wisp into your seas.
It's not my place to miss you, as *you*,
and it's not like you to want me to.

Pulled from the Valley;

After the strain of raw tendons, pulling
closed ends open;
after the sexual shock of will, and whim,
against meaty casts and tangible pangs
of twists and bends;
after a forsaken design of evidence, omitted;
a capitalistic casualty of natural parameters;
lifetimes enslaving lifetimes of civilized amateurs;
the readers of Dead Names and rotten faces brace
the burdens of rat races; for still,
we are not worth saving.
   Of what alien world, with angels and government,
              could a messiah deliver bells of serenity,
                         to apes so misplaced and
                                 malfunctioned?
Of what parallel lie could benevolent nothings
reach out from, like a brain
with a point,
to guarantee that
it's in us to make sense?

        This is our mission;
          our ship, our
             trip,
   and there will be no saviors.

        Why?

Doing to Be, Just Be;

Dare I say we are still asleep?
Dare I recommend a billion light reflections, to
invert back into our toiling frame, drear and
nightmarish... to see
that I'm still missing.
Dare we set ourselves aflame, and let the ashes
grow new garden grave-stone halos.

What of our precious life will show us now, the
light that beckons us to come back home?
What of that temptress, who pleads with one-
hundred and forty-four thousand tears, to follow
her back to a place so empty of all?

Some days are better, because the worst has been
given yet.
No day is worse, than the day all is forgiven,
yet what of hell is there if there's no heaven?
What do you stand on?
What do we stand in?
What do I *stand* for?

Death connects all things in meaning,
and I am but it's passenger.

I think we can move through time. Through
fate and pasts and resets, reset.
I've done it before; opened gates
to carry with white matter,

Secretions of the Beast

for when the loop
the cycle
the circle
the spiral
spins me 'round, and I say
Take me her again.

Take.

    Me.

        Here.

            Again.

                It's close, always... so close, always
so perfectly self-similar.
The pattern
in our fractal,
time.

I swear I love you, and I'm so sorry
to have to stir this cunning dream.
I can't stay for too long,
        my bones,
                      but I will give you all I grieve
in something beautiful; ineffable.
 In the death date of this birth; I swear I'll come
back home.

Φ

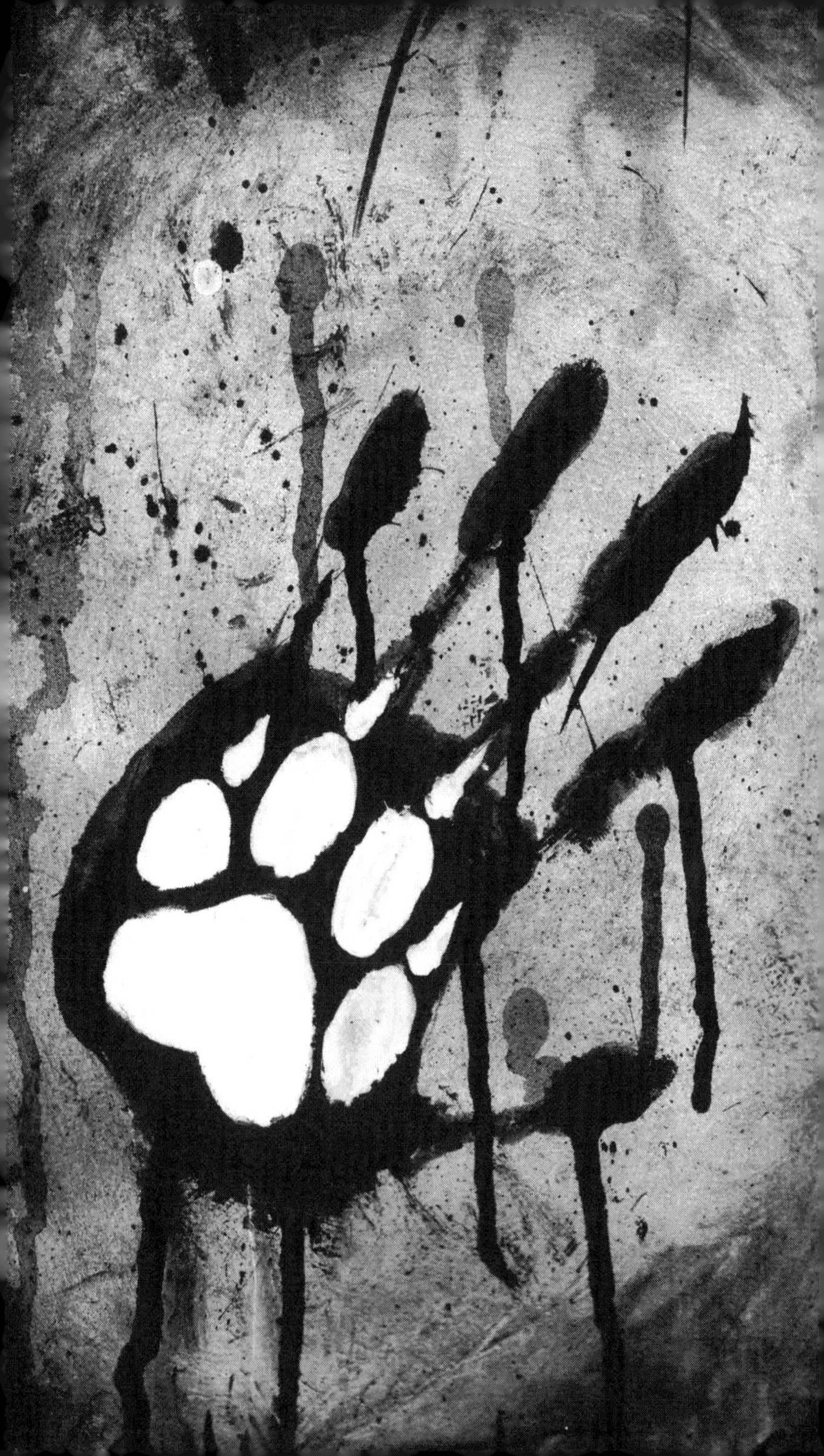

Secretions of the Beast

∞

An expression of gratitude

To the illustrative artists:

Charles Urban, page 6, 12, 35, 77-78.

Barry Kidwell, intro-page, page 31, 42, 75, 89.

Gabriell Quinn Pitcher, page 27, 49, 69.

To those who've offered their words to the world:

Marilyn Manson, 'Superstar Antichrist,' page 1.

Gene Wilder, 'Young Frankenstein' page 10-11.

Karl Marx, page 84.

To the reader, for supporting the craft that found, and saved me:

- : Emenual Wolff

- : @earthisanisland

- : @Emenwritings

∞

About the Author:

Emenual Wolff harbors no fear in addressing the dark, taboo, poignant, and raw spectrum of objective reality, animal emotion, and consciousness; the three of which he believes interact perpetually in constructing the nightmare thing, 'life.' His earlier work of poetry, 'MooNlight Howling,' has sold to three countries, striking unmovable existential dread in each of his readers. When he isn't writing, he's delivering spoken word performances in ways rather showy, yet recluse, behind masks, heavy face paints, robes, and more. As he puts it, 'I'm more than just a face.'
Being a strong believer in 'the mission of art,' he pushes his fellow artists to practice, exhibit, and sell their specific craft alongside him, and advocates for safe, non-discriminative spaces for all walks of artistic life. It's his hope that, through his craft, he can convince the reader that their feelings are valid, and that they are not alone. He aims to place his readers outside of and beside themselves, so as to initiate novel musings, and allow the chance for change to act upon their lives.

"There is a whole spectrum of healthy, human emotion that we are all entitled to feel at any given time. I'm here to remind people that evil exists in all things, especially the good. I'm here to remind them that great things can come from dark places..."
"...With supreme passion, and evidence, go."
-Emenual Wolff.

∞

Made in the USA
Lexington, KY
29 May 2018